WHAT IS THE BIBLE?

A Popular Introduction to the Greatest Book Ever Written

Robert R. Barr

WINSTON PRESS

Library of Congress Catalog Card Number: 83-51385

ISBN: 0-86683-727-2

Printed in the United States of America

5   4   3   2   1

Winston Press, Inc.
430 Oak Grove
Minneapolis, Minnesota 55403

Pronunciation symbols

ā Long vowel sound, as in bāke, ēasy, flōw

ä Changed vowel sound, as in cot, cart

ü Changed vowel sound, as in youth, cue

ĕ Unstressed vowel (schwa), as in banana, abut, America

´ Stressed syllable, as in aǵree, ḿemory

Contents

Chapter 1: How the Bible Came to Be 1
  A Whole Bundle of Books 1
  Two Testaments 2
  Oral Tradition 4
  The Patriarchal Society 6
  From Oral Tradition to Written Tradition 7
  The Community as Redactor 8
  The First Manuscripts 9
  Canonicity 12

Chapter 2: The Old Testament 15
  The Importance of Scholarship 15
  The Old Testament 17
  The Torah 18
  Compilations 21
  The Prophets 27
  The Great Historical Books 28
  Isaiah, Jeremiah, and Ezekiel 29
  The Writings 32
  The Apocrypha 34

Chapter 3: The New Testament 37
  The Good News 38
  The Parts of the New Testament 39
  The Four Gospels 41
  Dozens of "Gospels" 43
  The Authors of the Gospels 44
  The Synoptic Gospels 47
  The Gospel According to Mark 48
  The Gospel According to Matthew 52
  The Gospel According to Luke 56

The Fourth Gospel 58
The Acts of the Apostles 59
The Letters of the New Testament 61
The Letters of Saint Paul 61
The Other Letters 68
The Book of Revelation 70

Chapter 4: From Quill to Printing Press:
The World's Best-Seller 73
Manuscripts—"Written by Hand" 74
Manuscript History of the Hebrew Bible....... 77
The Qumran Scrolls 82
Printed Hebrew Bibles 84
The Septuagint 85
Six-Ply Bible of the Man of Steel 87
Latin Translations of the Old Testament 91
English Translations of the Bible............. 94
And Translations and Translations........... 98

Chapter 5: Word of God,
Word of Human Beings 99
Literary Genre 101
Inspiration and Errors in the Bible........... 106

Epilogue 112
Lord, I Have Loved Your Law 112
Lesson from Jews 112
Lesson from Eastern Christians 114
Lesson from Catholics..................... 116
Lesson from Protestants.................... 117

1
How the Bible Came to Be

The Bible is the story of our first creation, in Adam. It is the story of our "second creation" or re-creation, when God made us over again in Jesus Christ, his Son, who came to save us from our sins and lead us to everlasting life. And it is the story of where the world is headed.

It is also the story of our adventures with God in between. We human beings seem always to have had a hard time growing up. We are assailed by difficulties from all sides—and especially from within, for we are weak and selfish. The human race seems always to be a step behind where God wants it to be, so he pulls it along, by his love and his grace. The Bible is the story of these battles—battles that God has never been willing to let us fight alone. We might lose! So he has always come to our rescue. "The Lord God himself will fight for you," the Bible says. Why? Well, the Bible is a love story, too. . . .

A Whole Bundle of Books

And so the Bible is a story, a very special story. It must be a long story, too, you are probably thinking, because it is certainly a very thick book!

Indeed it is a long story. In fact, it is many "stories." God has a good many things to tell us for our "salvation," for our rescue, and he did not try to squeeze them all into a pamphlet. There is history in the Bible, and adventure; there are prayers, there is legend, there is prophecy, there are laws, there are lovely songs and poems, there are sermons, there are letters, there are visions. . . . There are all sorts of things God wants us to know, and so there are all sorts of things in the Bible, and many ways of telling them. In fact, all the information necessary for our salvation is right there in the Bible in one way or another.

If you were to pick up a bible and begin to page through it, you might notice something rather curious. One of the things you would probably see is that many little parts of the Bible are entitled "The Book of . . ." something or other, or somebody or other. And you would think, "*Of course* the Bible is a big book. It is a whole bundle of books!"

And you would be absolutely right. The Bible *is* a bundle of books—seventy-three of them! For, as we have just seen, God not only has many things to tell us in the Bible, but many *ways of telling them.* And so, in his wisdom, he assigned the writing of them to *many different authors.* Each author wrote just one book, or just a few books—or even just part of a book.

And each author wrote in his own particular style. Some were good at history, so they wrote history. Some were good at legends, so they wrote legends they had heard—legends packed with truth! Some were good at writing songs—like King David, who wrote some of the songs, called psalms. But all wrote truth, the truth God knows we need for our salvation.

Two Testaments

The Bible, then, is a bundle of books. Now, some of these books were written before Jesus came, and some after. Christians call the ones written before he came the "Old Testament," and the ones written after he came the "New Testament."

The Old Testament is the first part of the Bible. It is the longer part, about three-fourths of the whole Bible. It contains forty-six books. It was written during the period from about 900 B.C. to about 150 years before the birth of Christ. It was written mostly in Hebrew; but the later books were written in the languages that the Hebrew people had recently come to speak: Aramaic (which is like Hebrew), and Greek (the international language of the Roman Empire, that new world community, the "circle of lands" around the Mediterranean Sea).

The New Testament is the shorter, second part of the Bible, about one-fourth of it. It contains twenty-seven books. It was written shortly after Jesus' death and resurrection, mostly during the second half of the first century A.D. It was written entirely in Greek.

A "testament" is an official document bearing "testimony," or witness, that some legal act has been performed. For instance, if a person legally and officially declares what is to be done with his or her goods after he or she has died, the official legal document testifying to this is called a "Last Will and Testament." The Old and New Testaments, which together make up the Bible, are the documents of God's contracts with his people. For God has indeed entered into contracts with his people, called "covenants" (kĕv-ĕ-nĕnt), as we shall see.

And so it took about a thousand years for the Bible to be written by about forty different authors, all the way from Babylon (báb-ĕ-län) to Rome, about two thousand miles apart. Babylon was a great city in today's Iraq, in the Middle East. Rome is the capital of today's Italy.

Oral Tradition

How did the various books of the Bible come to be?

None of them was composed "of whole cloth," as the expression goes—by somebody sitting down and putting his feet up and his quill to his lips and saying, "Now, let's see, what shall I write?" Every book of the Bible—except the Letters of the New Testament, of course—is someone's earnest, urgent report of *what he has heard from someone else.*

In other words, each book of the Bible (except the Letters) originated in "oral tradition." The word "tradition" here is being used in its original meaning, as "a handing down." Oral tradition, then, is a handing down by word of mouth. These books were *spoken* before they were written.

In the case of most of the books of the Old Testament, the persons who first wrote them down had heard them from someone else, who had heard them from someone else, who had heard them from someone else . . . for time out of mind—for longer than anyone could remember.

A culture or civilization characterized by oral tradition is hard for us to recapture realistically today. We live in the "Gutenberg era," the age of the printed word, named after the man who supposedly invented printing by movable type in the A.D. 1400s. Indeed, to some people we seem to be entering a "post-Gutenberg" era, an age of electronic communication—telegraph, telephone, radio, and television—an age that will perhaps eventually de-emphasize the printed word until it almost disappears. In any case, we certainly no longer live in

4

times when the only way for news, or any other information, to travel was viva voce, word of mouth—person to person, living and present.

But most of the books of the Bible were first composed in an age of oral tradition, when all information was transmitted by word of mouth. In any case, almost no one could read or write in those days. There is an important cultural difference between us today and the men and women who first handed down, orally, the words we read on paper today in the Bible. (A "cultural difference" is a difference in the way people of different times or places think and feel, a difference in what they know about the world and about themselves, a difference in their "values," or what they think is important in life, and so on.) One cultural difference between us and the people who first composed the words of the Bible is a huge one: *literacy,* the ability to read and write.

To put it another way—most of the books of the Bible were originally composed not on paper but in people's heads. Then they were recited, and recited, and recited again, from generation to generation, until they were *eventually* written down.

Perhaps the closest most of us ever come to a culture of oral tradition would be the precious moments we may have enjoyed around a campfire in the evening, or before a fireplace, listening to . . . perhaps stories people tell, things that have actually happened to them, things that they have heard really happened, simply made-up stories or songs or "poems," or perhaps verses about fabulous people in our family long ago. Practically every different kind of these oral traditions is represented in the books of the Bible. But what a tiny taste of oral tradition, our few evenings spent in front of the fire! In ancient times, when the books of the Bible were first composed in people's heads, *all* information was communicated by word of mouth.

The Patriarchal Society

Another cultural difference between us today and people of two or three thousand years ago is that they almost always lived in a patriarchal society. The word "patriarch" comes from the Greek *patr-,* "father," and *-archēs,* "leader." The father was absolute head of the *family.* His word was law. His word was also wisdom. The only one he looked up to was *his* father. As a result, since extended families stayed much closer together in those days than they do today, a whole extended family, or *clan,* would live its whole life gathered in spirit (and also in body) around the grandfather, or even the great-grandfather, of them all. He was the patriarch. He was the great leader, everybody's "father," and his word was law and wisdom.

Then, just as a group of families, each under the headship of a father, made up a clan, under the great-grandfather, or patriarch, so a group of clans would join together into a *tribe* so that they could share the duties of hunting and gathering, or later farming, and self-defense. And who was the head of the tribe? All the patriarchs of all the clans, perhaps. Or some of the most outstanding of them. Or perhaps one of their number would be considered even more worthy of reverence and obedience than the others; then he would be chieftain of the whole tribe.

This, then, completes our picture of how most of the books of the Bible came to be composed: in oral tradition in a patriarchal society: whole clans sitting around the same campfire, or around the same spring in the same oasis after a hard day's desert journey, listening to the patriarch recite history, tell stories, sing, recite love poetry he knew from the days of his youth—everything anyone in the tribe, from the children on up, could ever hope to learn. For remember, there was no television, no radio, no telephone, no books or newspapers. There were not even any schools. People could not read or write. There was just the family, the clan, and the tribe to *tell* them what they needed to know.

This is how all ancient literature began—the epic literature of Greece, for instance, the *Iliad* and the *Odyssey,* or the great Scandinavian sagas—by oral tradition. This, by the way, is why so much ancient literature, including many parts of the Bible, is in the form of poetry. Words in verse are easier to remember and also are more suitable for group recitation and singing.

From Oral Tradition to Written Tradition

But evidently, what had been handed down in oral tradition from generation to generation must have been put in writing one fine day. For of course the Bible today is in writing.

We do not know who first wrote down any of the books of the Old Testament, that is, who first wrote down what he or she had heard in oral tradition. Today the authors of the Old Testament are anonymous, meaning nameless.

But we know *someone* must have reworked the oral tradition into writing—"redacted" it, as we say, using the word we have from Latin for "reworked." So we refer to this unknown person simply as the "original, anonymous redactor."

The Community as Redactor

We do not know what *individuals,* then, made any of these "first redactions"—wrote any parts of the Old Testament down for the first time—any more than we know the names or identity of the heads of families who handed them down in oral tradition. But here an important point has to be made: At least we know that in a very real way it was the *whole community* that redacted any part of the Bible. The books of the Bible, as we have them today, or any of their parts, must have been *interesting and important to a large number of people,* or they would not have survived these thousands of years.

Why is this point so important? The Bible is the word of God. And the *word of God is addressed to a people,* a community. The Old Testament is God's word to the ancient people of Israel. The New Testament is God's word to the primitive Christian community, the very first Christians, who lived in the time of the apostles. The words of the Bible may not have been *originally* addressed to a whole community. They may be, for example, the words of a particular prophet to his little circle of followers. But the word of God was *eventually* received by the whole community. This is why it survived in so many tellings, then in so much writing, all these thousands of years.

In other words, whoever the original anonymous redactor was, he was writing what was destined to be much read and much loved by a large community. Possibly he even knew this, or at least suspected it, at the time he was writing, and this was why he wrote. Or possibly he did not know it. But in either case, what he wrote *was* preserved by the community, for it did become popular enough to survive right down to our day.

This is why we can say, regardless of who the original redactor was, that it was the community who effectively redacted any part of the Bible, by being the kind of community that would "like" the book that an individual was redacting.

And so the original redactor of the books of the Old Testament turns out to be not so unknown after all. It was the people of Israel, the ancient Hebrews, the twelve tribes of Israel, who had passed down something interesting from generation to generation in oral tradition in some of their families and then were pleased to see it in writing. That meant that it could be read to all the people, since some people had learned to read.

The original redactor of the new Testament, too, turns out to be not so anonymous after all. For regardless of what individual first wrote down the things he or she had heard about Jesus from the apostles, that original redactor was the early Christian community of the second half of the first century A.D., who had been hearing these things by word of mouth for several years now and were glad to see them in writing. For this, they knew, was the word of God to them.

The First Manuscripts

Just as we do not know today who the original *individual* redactors of most of the parts of the Bible were, so also in no case do we have any of the original "manuscripts" of the Bible (from the Latin *manu-*, "by hand," and *-script*, "written"). Each was doubtless either a piece or a number of pieces of that ancestor of paper called "papyrus" (pĕ-pī-rĕs); or perhaps in some cases it was etched, that is, scratched into clay "tablets." But either way, those manuscripts have long since crumbled to dust. Neither papyrus nor clay could stay in good condition for Two or three thousand years. Even most of today's paper couldn't.

But the books of the Bible must have survived somehow. After all, here they are today, nicely bound, on your shelf at home. How did they survive, if their original manuscripts have crumbled to dust?

The answer is that before each original manuscript deteriorated to the point of being unreadable, it was copied onto new papyrus or new clay. And then *that* manuscript was copied, before *it* crumbled, and so on, down to the invention of printing in the early part of the fifteenth century A.D.

If the person copying a manuscript *merely* copied it, without making any deliberate major changes, then he is called a "copyist." (Of course, he may have made mistakes, at least little ones, as any of us would in copying a long manuscript.) But if he deliberately *reworked* the text, changing things here and there to what seemed to him to be a clearer or better or truer way to say the same thing in a significantly different way, then he is called—you guessed it—a redactor.

Who were these subsequent redactors? Again, just as with the original redactor, we do not know who these individuals were. But here too, as with the original redactors, we do know that it was the whole community—the people or part of the people of Israel for the Old Testament, and the earliest Christian communities for the New Testament—who came to accept these writings as the Word of God, and came to accept them *in this or that particular redaction.* Thus we say that *it was the early communities who made not only the original redaction but all the subsequent ones as well.*

The whole process of handing down, in ancient times, a story, history, poem, or the like, is called "tradition." Oral tradition, or handing-down, consists in transmitting a literary work *by word of mouth* from generation to generation, from patriarch to the younger members of the family, then from them, when they grew old, to the younger members of *their* families. So also "written tradition," or handing-down-in-writing, consists of the transmission of a literary work (indeed perhaps the very same one that has been handed down in oral tradition from generation to generation) in *manuscript* form, that is, from clay to papyrus (when papyrus had been invented) to parchment (when *it* had been invented).

Papyrus and parchment scrolls were very handy to use and store. They needed to be finished smooth on only one side—the inside of what would become the scroll, the side that would be written upon—and then glued or sewn into a long sheet, rolled up into a scroll, and unrolled gradually to be written upon. When filled with writing, the scroll was rolled up and put away. When needed, it could be unrolled to just the place to be read from, and then gradually unrolled from one end and rolled up from the other as the reading progressed.

The Bible was preserved on papyrus and

parchment scrolls for two thousand years on copy after copy as long as the scroll copied from could still be read. This process went on until the invention of printing.

Now our picture of the original composition and transmission of the Bible is complete. It began in oral tradition and has continued in written tradition down to our own day.

Canonicity

But one problem remains. Today we think of the Bible as one book. But it was originally composed, and eventually written down, in the form of many books. Who grouped these books together? Who arranged the books of the prophets into one long series of books? Who put the New Testament letters together and decided in what order they should appear? And who put *all* the books of the Old and New Testaments together into one big book, the Bible?

Again, we do not know which individuals did these things. Again, for all practical purposes, the whole community did them. For here too, as in the case of all the redactions, the Bible had to be written in such a way that it would be read and used, or it would not have survived.

And so, as it became clearer and clearer to the community—first the ancient people of Israel before Jesus came and then the early Christian communities— that *these books were considered sacred, the word of God to them,* individuals within the community began to write *lists of which books were holy.*

These lists are called "canons," from the old Greek word for a rod, or measuring stick—the "norm," the "rule," the measuring stick for which books were the holy books.

You see, as long as books were still on scrolls and not on pages, only a single book of the Bible (if it was a long one) or several short ones could be rolled up into one. A person could not handle one scroll hundreds of feet long, all rolled up into one; and so the Bible could not be all on one scroll. Therefore, to see which scrolls, which books, belonged to the group of holy books, one had to look at a canon—one of the lists of sacred books which someone had drawn up.

These canons differed from one another over the centuries because individuals or communities did not always agree on which books were sacred. Eventually, though, general agreement was reached for most parts of the Bible. That is, the canon was "fixed"; after that it no longer changed.

For example, shortly after Jesus' resurrection, enthusiasm for him ran so high that *dozens* of "gospels," not just four, were written. One of them emphasizes Jesus' childhood very strongly, and contains this story: One day the child Jesus and his playmates were fashioning birds out of clay. The game developed into a contest to see which child's bird was most like a real one. Well, little Jesus won the contest very handily—when his bird was finished, he blessed it and it flew away!

But you will not read this cute little story in any of the Gospels today. Why? Because even though *some* people originally thought that this sort of game-playing could be the word of God to them, eventually *the Christian community as a whole* did not think their Lord and Savior would have used that kind of magic "trick"—not even on his playmates. So they rejected this gospel as false. They rejected other gospels as well—dozens of them. Finally, when the Christian community agreed in the fourth century on an official list of twenty-seven New Testament books, the list or canon included only four gospels, the four we have today: Matthew, Mark, Luke, and John. Thus we say, "The New Testament canon was fixed in the fourth century."

Books considered to be God's word are placed on these official lists or canons and therefore are called the "canonical" books or are said to have "canonicity."

Now the Christians had decided on their canon of the New Testament. They had also decided which Jewish canon of the Old Testament they would accept. (As we shall see in Chapter 2, there was some question, even among Jews, about whether some of the books of the Old Testament as we have it today really belonged in it.) So the forty-six canonical books of the Old Testament were then joined to the twenty-seven canonical Books of the New Testament to form one "corpus," or body, of sacred literature, seventy-three books in all.

All these dozens of sacred books were faithfully written out on *biblia*, or scrolls. They were copied from others before them and then rolled up and kept in a place of special reverence, where they could be unrolled and studied, or read to the people during the celebration of the Eucharist. Thus the Bible was born.

2
The Old Testament

The Importance of Scholarship

Much of the Bible was written more than 2,000 years ago in the Middle East. No book written that long ago and far away could possibly be easy for us to pick up and read here and now. People's languages were different from ours, and they thought differently—their "culture" was different from ours.

In order to be properly understood by people today, the Bible has to be studied scientifically. The men and women who do this scientific study are called "Bible scholars" or "Scripture scholars."

The first thing Scripture scholars have to do is learn the languages in which the Bible was mainly written—Hebrew and Greek. Hebrew is very different from English. Generally its words bear no similarity to ours. Even its alphabet is not the same as ours, and if you saw a page of Hebrew for the first time you would be unable to recognize a single letter, let alone a whole word.

And it would not be of much help to you to be told that Hebrew is to be read "backwards"—from right to left instead of from left to right. (Of course, this does not seem backwards to a person who is used to reading Hebrew. In fact, he or she might well wonder why *we* read and write "backwards"!)

Biblical Greek, on the other hand, is not terribly hard for English-speaking people to learn. The Greek alphabet may *look* very different from ours at first glance. But that is because its "script" is a little different, just as one person's "script," or handwriting, may differ from another person's, even when they are writing the same letters and words. Actually, the Greek alphabet is similar to ours—in fact, ours comes from it—and you could probably learn it in about an hour. Then, with proper instruction, you could probably learn enough biblical Greek in just a dozen evenings or so to enjoy comparing your English New Testament with the original Greek. Who knows? This might be one of the pleasures in store for you some day, even without being a full-fledged Scripture scholar.

Or maybe this is not something you will do. No one has the time or interest for everything. But even if we ourselves do not learn Hebrew and Greek, it is a good thing *someone* does. It is a good thing there are Scripture scholars, who teach in the universities, dig in the caves of the Holy Land, or write books *about* the great book, the Bible. For it is not only the languages of the Bible that are different from ours. There are many other differences, too, between us and the people that lived two thousand years ago on the other side of the world. There are great cultural differences. Cultural differences, remember, are the differences in the way people of different times or places think, feel, and act, because that is the way they have been brought up to think, feel, and act. And if it were not for Scripture scholars, who learn all they can about the people of the Bible and the way they thought and felt and spoke—and especially the way they wrote books!—we would have a difficult time indeed understanding the Bible. But thanks to Scripture scholars and the things they tell us, we actually know far more about the Bible, even though it was written so long ago and so far away, than we know about any other book that was ever written.

The Bible is the number one best seller of all time. No other book in the history of the world has been found as interesting by so many millions of people. That is why it has been studied so much.

The little book that you are holding in your hands right now—this little book about the great book—has been written in order to bring you some of the things Scripture scholars have discovered and passed on to us.

The Old Testament

Now that we have seen something of how the Bible *in general* came to be, let us look at its *particular parts* more closely.

As we have seen, the Bible is in two main parts. The longer part comes first and is called the Old Testament. The shorter part comes at the end and is called the New Testament. The Old Testament comes from the oral tradition and written redactions of the ancient people of Israel. The New Testament comes from the oral tradition and written redactions of the very first Christians.

This chapter will be about the Old Testament.

The Old Testament is the first three-fourths of the Bible. It contains forty-six of the Bible's seventy-three books.

The thirty-nine Hebrew books of the Old Testament are further subdivided by Jews into (1) the Books of the Torah (tór-ĕ), (2) the Books of the Prophets, and (3) the Writings.

The Torah consists of the first five books of the Old Testament—the first five books of the Bible. What are the names of these books?

In Hebrew, the name of a book of the Bible is simply the first word of that book. For example, the Hebrew name for the first Book of the Bible is *Bereshith,* meaning, "In the beginning." For this is how the first book of the Bible starts out. It is as if we called our national anthem, not "The Star-Spangled Banner" but "O Say, Can You See." There were not nearly as many books in ancient times as there are today, so it was easy to identify them from the words with which they began.

But Jews just before the time of Jesus, and Christians after them, had begun to speak Greek, the international language of their part of the world. So they had the Bible translated from Hebrew into Greek, and as they did so, they gave the books of the Bible Greek names. It is these Greek names, or their Latin or English translations, that we still use today.

The first Book of the Torah, then, is called the **Book of Genesis.** *Genesis* (Gén-ĕ-sĕs) is the old Greek word for "origin," or beginning. It is an English word as well, meaning practically the same thing. The reason for calling this book the Book of Genesis is that it is about the creation of the world and the origin of the Jewish people.

The second Book of the Torah is called the **Book of Exodus.** *Exodus* (éx-ĕ-dĕs) is the old Greek word for "exit," or "going out." This name is given to it because it is the story of the Jews' "going out" of the land of Egypt, when they escaped from slavery to freedom across the waters of the sea under the leadership of Moses. It describes the first two years of the forty years they spent in the desert of the Sinai (sī-nī) before they got to the Promised Land of Canaan (Kā-nĕn).

The third Book of the Torah is called the **Book of Leviticus** (lĕ-vít-i-kĕs), meaning "pertaining to the Levites" (lĕ-vīts). A priest in ancient Hebrew times who offered sacrifice in the Temple at Jerusalem had to be a Levite—a descendant or member of the tribe of Levi. The third book of the Bible is filled with rules and laws for Temple worship—rules and laws for Levites, then. Hence it is called Leviticus, meaning the Levites' Book.

The fourth Book of the Torah is called the **Book of Numbers** because of the two censuses that were taken of the people of Israel during their wanderings in the desert of the Sinai. These two censuses are reported in this fourth book of the Bible, one at the beginning and the other near the end. This book also recounts the wanderings themselves, which lasted for thirty-eight years. Including the two years encamped at the foot of Mount Sinai, they spent forty years, all told, in the desert. Their wanderings ended when they came to the Promised Land of Canaan.

The fifth Book of the Torah is called the **Book of Deuteronomy** (dyū-ter-ä-nĕ-mē), from the Greek *deutero-*, "second," and *-nom-*, "law." This book reports a "second time" the laws God gave to Moses and the people while they were encamped at the foot of Mount Sinai after their escape from Egypt. The Book of Deuteronomy also retells some of what happened at the very end of the Jews' sojourn in the desert, before they reached the Promised Land. Many of the books of the Bible repeat one another, somewhat, and we shall soon see why.

These five books, then, the first five books of the Bible—Genesis, Exodus, Leviticus, Numbers, and Deuteronomy—make up the Torah. The canon of the Torah was fixed by the time of the Babylonian (bäb-ĕ-lō-nē-ĕn) Exile. This was the period during which the Jewish upper classes were in slavery in neighboring Babylon (bäb-ĕ-län), in today's Iraq. They had been deported to this land by their Babylonian conquerors in 587-86 B.C., and they stayed there into the next century. It is easy to see why the Jews would have loved and needed the great story of their rescue from the land of Egypt centuries before. For now they were in captivity and slavery again, in another foreign land—only to the north this time, instead of to the south. But Yahweh, the God who had delivered them from Egypt, was still their God today; and surely he would deliver them from Babylon, too! (And he did.)

Christians often call the Torah the "Pentateuch" (pén-tĕ-tyūk) from the Greek *pent-,* "five," and *-teuch,* "volume," because it is a five-volume shelf of books, so to speak. Jews often call these five books the "Books of Moses," because it used to be thought that Moses had written them all personally. But we shall call them by their principal Jewish name, the Torah, the Hebrew word for "law." For it is in these five books that the laws God gave Moses are reported.

The Old Testament is sometimes called the Old Covenant. A covenant is a sacred contract or agreement that someone will do something for someone else. In the Book of Genesis, God makes a covenant with Abraham: He promises to multiply Abraham's offspring—his children and his children's children—as the stars in the sky or the sands of the seashore. And so Abraham becomes the great patriarch of the whole Jewish people.

Now, if the canon of the Torah was fixed in the sixth or fifth century B.C., we know that its written tradition must have been redacted before that, and its oral tradition before that. How did these redactions take place?

Compilations

Each book of the Torah, like so many books of the Bible, is a "compilation" or collection of different writings, strung together by their unknown final redactor in a way that seemed to him would make the most sense. For example, if you look closely, you can easily see that the first book of the Bible, the Book of Genesis, tells the story of the creation of the world *twice*. The first story begins with the opening words of the Bible: "In the beginning, when God created the heavens and the earth . . ." and goes through Chapter One, then into the beginning of Chapter Two. But in the middle of verse four of Chapter Two, the story of creation stops: "Such is the story of the heavens and the earth at their creation."

And at once the story of creation starts all over again! Right in the middle of verse four of Chapter Two of the Book of Genesis, after ". . . at their creation," we read: "At the time when the Lord God made the earth and the heavens—while as yet there was no field shrub on earth. . . ." And then the story starts all over again, and goes to the end of the chapter. Only it is in different words this time!

How did this happen? Evidently the final redactor,

before the Torah canon was fixed, thought the two stories too good to choose between. Each was too full of truth to leave out. Each had details the other hadn't; but the redactor didn't want to blend them into one, probably because he felt this would be changing them, and that he shouldn't change such important things. So he strung both stories of creation together.

But then why does the first creation story stop, and the second start, in such a strange place—in the middle of a verse? Why not at the end of a chapter? That would be a much more logical dividing place.

None of the books of the Bible was originally divided into chapters and verses. Each of them just started at the start and ended at the end, like a newspaper article. Only many centuries later did a certain Christian "monk" (a member of a very old religious community of men) decide to mark up his copy of the Bible with chapter numbers and verse numbers so that it would be easier to keep a record of exactly where this or that was said in the Bible. Now, our monk may have worked very fast. He had hundreds of chapters and thousands of verses to mark off. In any case, he seems not to have noticed that he was breaking Chapters One and Two of Genesis not where one story ends and the other starts, but a few lines before the end of the first. He would probably be the first to agree with us that Chapter One should have gone on a little longer and then be broken.

But what is important is that these are two different stories of creation in two different styles. They say different things about creation. Here is one important example: In the first creation story, man and woman are seen in something very much like equality with one another. In fact, maleness and femaleness added together are seen as what makes the human being the image of God!

God created man in his image;
in the divine image he created him;
male and female he created them.

But in the second creation story, woman is formed from a rib God takes from the man's side, so that she seems much inferior to him.

It is interesting that the second story is much older than the first.

This is an excellent example of the *multiple authorship* of one and the same book of the Bible. Just as the whole Bible is made up of many books by many authors, so too, especially in the Old Testament, a single book as we have it today may be a compilation of writings on more or less the same subject by different (and usually anonymous) authors. Of course, it is oral tradition that provides each of these original authors, these original redactors, with the information he is writing about. For example, the first redactor of the first creation story, Chapter One of Genesis, redacts on clay or papyrus what has been handed down to him "around the campfire," so to speak, for many generations. Then a second redactor comes along and *joins* this to, say, several other writings about creation. Then a third redactor, a generation or two later, might *add* some oral material *he* has heard in *his* family, something not in any of the writings joined together by the second redactor—perhaps just a few lines here and there to cement them together. Then still another redactor might *subtract* something he thinks is unnecessary from the version going onto the papyrus he is writing or dictating. Then still another might simply *switch* some sections around a bit, in such a way as to make more sense to him, or because that was the way he had heard it in *his* family's oral tradition. Or perhaps only some of these things happened in the various redactions of a given book. Or perhaps they all happened, or almost all, but in a different order.

It is the task of Scripture scholars to try to figure out how each book of the Bible is twined together—to try to discern which unknown redactor did what. They do this by examining both "internal evidence" and "external evidence." The "internal evidence" for their conclusions consists in what is found in the *book itself*—a switch in styles of writing for instance, like the sudden appearance of the name "Yahweh" for God instead of "the Lord." The "external evidence" consists in what scholars know from *sources outside* the book—what we know from the history books of other nations, for instance.

Again, in our example, it is easy to see from the "internal evidence"—just the way the words are—that one creation story stops and another starts right in the middle of a verse.

So the Book of Genesis, like other books of the Bible, was redacted and redacted and redacted, until . . . when? When did the redacting of the written tradition stop?

The last redaction of any book of the Bible must have taken place before its canon was fixed. For example, in the case of the Torah, the last redaction of each of the five books must have been completed before the time of the Babylonian Captivity, since that was when the canon of the Torah was fixed.

However many redactions there may have been before that—however much the Book of Genesis, for instance, may have changed from the time of its oral tradition to the time of the Babylonian Captivity—evidently some redactor came along whose version met with general community acceptance in Israel.

For when a canon is fixed, its books are "frozen," so to speak. A canon is fixed only because now the community feels that these books are very important for their religion. And when people feel that something is important for their religion, generally they don't like to see changes made. This is why, generally speaking, all the stringing together and adding and subtracting and switching around and any other changing that goes on in the books of the Bible happens *before* canonization, that is, before the canon is fixed.

Now we have had a good look at the multiple authorship of the Bible, or even of one book of the Bible. And now we can understand why, for instance, some of the books of the Bible repeat things that other books of the Bible have said, and repeat them in a different way, as we have seen in several books of the Torah. The reason is that all the books of the Bible were redacted separately and several times in their written tradition before they became "frozen" as their canon was fixed. The redactors of one book often had no way of knowing what the redactors of another book were doing. And when the community came to fix the canon, they took each book just as it was at that moment, and put them all together into a group of sacred books—the beginnings of the Bible. So naturally there was some repetition.

The multiple authorship of the Bible can also help us understand why what comes first in a book is not necessarily the first thing to have been actually written in that book. The reason is that the redactors switched things around in such a way as to seem to make the best sense, without regard, often, to where their material had come from nor, of course, how old its various parts were.

Now, if *part* of a book can be older than the part just before it, as is the case with the first two chapters of the Book of Genesis, it must be easy for a whole book to be older than the books coming before it in any canon, or list of books. Here again we have a good example in the Torah: Genesis is not the oldest book of the Torah, hence not the oldest book of the Bible, even though it is the first.

Why did the community slip it in first? Clearly because the Book of Genesis is, as its name implies, the story of origins. What actually happened was this: The Hebrews already had the Book of Exodus, and other books, all concerned with the history of their people. Now, they began to wonder, what happened before that? How did their people come to be in the first place? How did the human race come to be? How did the whole world come to be? And the redactors, wondering the same things, set to work. They began to write down what they had heard in their families' oral tradition about the creation of the world and the beginnings of the Hebrew people. The result was the Book of Genesis *after* many other books had been redacted. But when the canon of the Torah was fixed, Genesis was inserted in front of all the other books because it was about *beginnings.*

Once the canon of the Torah had been fixed, the redactions stopped. From that day to this, the Torah has remained the same for 2,500 years.

The Prophets

The Hebrew Old Testament, as we saw, was divided into Torah, Prophets, and "Writings."

The twenty-two books called the Books of the Prophets were in turn divided into two sets of books called the "Former Prophets" (the earlier books) and the "Latter Prophets" (the later books).

The Former Prophets do not strike us today as books of prophecy at all. They are the history and legends of the Jewish people in the Promised Land of Canaan. And so nowadays these Former Prophets are often called "historical books," so that instead of having three divisions of the Bible, as the old Hebrews had—Law, Prophets, and Writings—today's Christians have four: the Law, the Historical Books, the Prophets, and the Writings.

After the Former Prophets come the truly prophetical books, the "Latter Prophets." The books of the Latter Prophets are the Books of Isaiah, Jeremiah, Lamentations, and Ezekiel. Then come the twelve "Minor" Prophets—so called not because these prophets themselves are unimportant, but because their twelve books are so short they could all fit on one scroll.

Let us take a brief look at each of these three divisions: (1) the great historical books, (2) the four great prophets, and (3) the twelve minor prophets.

The books of history and legend, which the Hebrews called the Former Prophets, came right after the five books of the Torah and are six in number. They are called the Books of Joshua, Judges, Samuel, and Kings. (Samuel and Kings were soon divided into two scrolls each, so that for almost the whole time they have been in existence we have had the Books of Joshua, Judges, First Samuel, Second Samuel, First Kings, and Second Kings.) Their canon was fixed by the Hebrews less than a hundred years after the Torah canon was fixed, about the middle of the 400s B.C.

The **Book of Joshua** recounts the military exploits of the Hebrew people under Moses' successor, Joshua. Thus it spans only the length of one lifetime.

After Joshua died, the leadership of the people was taken over by a succession of twelve generals, who had the title of "Judge" because they ruled the people and saw that they obeyed the laws. The **Book of Judges** is the history of this period.

The **Books of Samuel** are about Samuel, the last judge-general, and his military and political battles. The judges are then replaced by kings. Saul was the first king and David the second; and Samuel used his influence to see that David did indeed become king.

The adventures recounted in these books are often wild and bloody. The reason they, and other books of violence in the Bible, were canonized is that the military victories of the Hebrews were always seen as a sign of God's favor. Today we would agree with the ancient Hebrews that our victories over evil, including oppression, are possible only because God is "fighting on our side." We would disagree with them, however, that God commands us to slaughter innocent civilians. That is, *today* we would disagree with them. Of course, if we had lived in their times, when practically every community in the world saw or experienced war and slaughter, and was enslaved or enslaved others, doubtless we would have agreed with them. The God of the Hebrews has stayed with us every minute, Christians believe, right up to the present day, and teaches us things today about love and peace that he did not teach so clearly in Old Testament times. And doubtless he has things still to teach future generations about world peace and love, things that even we do not yet suspect. God is still building his world.

After the Books of Samuel come the Books of Kings. The **Books of Kings** tell the history and legends of Israel from toward the end of the great King David's reign through all the kings after him, until the Babylonian Captivity of the 500s B.C. Very important among all these kings is King Solomon, and the Temple he built, where from then on the worship of God was to be officially performed.

Isaiah, Jeremiah, and Ezekiel

After the great historical books (the Former Prophets) come the books of the prophets, properly so called. Their canon was fixed by 200 B.C. at the latest.

The first part of the **Book of Isaiah** (ī-źā-ĕ) is a collection of mighty poems, composed by this greatest of all the prophets and some of his disciples. The second, very different, part of the same book was composed by an unknown poet two centuries later, toward the end of the Babylonian Exile, and is especially well known for its powerful, beautiful "Songs of the Servant of Yahweh"—the mysterious, loving Suffering Servant who died for our sins and was raised up somehow by God because he did so. Christians believe that the Servant prophecies are most perfectly fulfilled in Jesus.

The **Book of Jeremiah** recounts the warnings of the great leader and prophet of that name who lived in the 600s B.C. In his great poems Jeremiah explains to the people that their sufferings, especially at the hands of invaders who loved to torture and kill, were a result of their faithlessness to God. Of course, it is clear as well that God hates the awful doings of the invaders.

The Book of Jeremiah is a good example of what an Old Testament prophet was. Contrary to popular opinion, the task of a prophet or prophetess was *not mainly to foretell the future, but to explain the present.* "Prophet," then, from the Greek *pro-,* "forth," and *-phē-,* "speak, tell," does not mean to "fore-tell," but to "speak forth, speak out"—fearlessly, just because God commands him or her to speak out and tell the whole truth. A prophet feels *driven* to tell the whole truth, cost him or her what it may. Jeremiah, like so many of the prophets, had to suffer at the hands of the people who did not like what he had to tell them. Some—like Jeremiah himself, apparently—were even killed for telling the truth.

The **Book of Lamentations,** formerly called the Lamentations of Jeremiah, is a book of five touchingly sad songs by someone who actually saw Jerusalem fall to the Babylonians and many of the people driven away to Babylon to serve their conquerors. Israel, the Bride of God, the author says, has been brought low. And yet she has not lost her hope! God will come and deliver her.

The **Book of Ezekiel** is a particularly good example of the two things an Old Testament prophet did best. First, he warns the people that their sufferings are a result of their sins, which are so terrible, he says, that Jerusalem will be destroyed because of them. (So a prophet *does* foretell the future sometimes, but only because it is a result of the present. Mainly, the prophet is explaining the present, from God's viewpoint.) Second, Ezekiel explains, after Jerusalem is destroyed, God still loves his people and will make them happy and great again. A prophet, then, explains suffering as a result of sin and injustice, and happiness as a result of God's love for his people.

The minor prophets, like the four great prophets we have already seen, also beautifully remind people in their twelve short books that God's anger is not forever and that its purpose is never simply to destroy. God's anger is meant to heal, not harm. It is intended to help people stop being selfish and start being generous. It is intended to bring sinners back to God so that they can regain the happiness they lost when they became selfish.

Nowadays we know that God does not have emotions as human beings do, that God does not exactly "grow angry" with us and "punish" us. We know that he simply loves us, most tenderly, and that *we* punish *ourselves* by the cruelty and selfishness we spread around in the world as we turn our souls inside-out with greed instead of generously turning them outward, toward others. But in these early times, when people were even more crude and rough, often, than they are today and their emotions passionate for both good and evil, the prophets had found a good way to help people understand God's wish that they become as loving and generous as he himself: They painted poetic pictures of him as being just as emotional as his people.

The Writings

All the books of the Bible are "writings." True, most of them started in oral tradition. But they were all eventually redacted as writings. Then why call *some* of them "Writings"?

As we might suspect, this third and last category of the books of the Old Testament is simply a catchall for what does not fit into the other two categories, the Torah and the Prophets. Indeed, we find that the ancient Jews sometimes called the Writings simply "the rest of the books," or the "later authors," that is, any *biblia,* or scrolls, that were not Torah or Prophets.

Another reason, however, why this third and last category is "nameless," so to speak, is that its canon was fixed so late—apparently only two or three generations before Jesus, in the first century B.C.

Nowadays the Writings are usually called the "wisdom literature," because several of them are instructional books for Jewish boys to memorize— the forerunners of our parents' old catechisms. This is why several of these books are in verse: for easy memorizing. Doubtless Jesus memorized them, too, when he was a boy and could recite them all his life.

The wisdom literature (or Writings) wrestles with

such crucial problems as good and bad behavior, suffering, death, where we come from, and where we are going.

The instructional books are the **Books of Proverbs, Ecclesiastes,** and **Wisdom.** These are collections of sermonettes and sayings, mostly in poetry, which had become favorites of the people and their sages (those who were thought to know "what it was all about"). Here we learn about virtue and vice, fear of the Lord as the beginning of wisdom, how the young should treat their elders, and so on.

The other three books of the wisdom literature, or Writings, are among the most outstanding books in the whole Bible. The **Book of Job** tries to answer the problem of why innocent people suffer. The **Song of Songs** is a long, exquisitely lovely wedding song containing some of the tenderest and most intense love poetry in existence.

The **Book of Psalms,** of course, is the most remarkable of all the Writings. It is the most prayed book in the Bible. It is made up of 150 songs, whose melodies, unfortunately, have been lost, but whose words are music all by themselves.

There are many types of psalms. Some are written to be sung during worship in the Temple. Some are written for group prayer in other places. Some are for being prayed by an individual, in times of great sorrow, for instance. Some are long, and run on for pages. One is just two verses long.

One type of psalm sings the glory of the God who rescued his people from the land of Egypt. Another type praises God as the creator and lord of nature— earth, moon, stars, light, and storm. A third type praises God as king of his people. Another kind of psalm begs help in time of national crisis, and still another, for help in personal crisis. There are songs of sorrow for sin, there are psalms of faith, and there are songs of close, loving union with God. Finally, there are songs of a great king to come, who Christians believe must be Jesus Christ.

There is an old Jewish legend that, late one hot summer's night, King David was awakened from his fitful sleep by the sound of a midnight breeze playing on the strings of his harp. Enchanted by the sound, he arose and began to sing. All night through he "married the words to the sounds," and when the red of morning shone in the East, all 150 psalms were finished.

Surely David did write some of the psalms, but Scripture scholars have shown us that these were only some of the very early ones, that other musicians and poets wrote most of them later. But they are all in David's spirit of praying with one's whole self—mind, heart, and even body—in dance and song.

The Apocrypha

Some of the most beautiful and interesting books of the Old Testament are not in the Hebrew Bible at all. We have already seen that some Old Testament books were written later than the others, and in Greek or Aramaic. They were written after the canon of the Hebrew Old Testament—the Torah, Prophets, and Writings—was fixed (or in the process of being fixed, in the case of the Writings), just one or two centuries before Christ.

Some people have thought they are not the word of God at all. Others, like Martin Luther, have thought they are the word of God indeed, but surely not so sacred as the great old Hebrew Books. And so Luther included them in the Old Testament but grouped them together at the end as a kind of "second shelf" of books. And this is what "apocrypha" (ĕ-pä-krĕ-fĕ) means (from the Greek *apo-*, "away," and *-kryph-*, "hide"): "hidden," pushed back behind the others—the row of books behind the other books. Traditionally, Catholics believe these books are just as much inspired by God as the Torah, Prophets, or Writings, and just as important for our salvation.

Nowadays, both Catholics and Protestants often place these later books here and there all through the Old Testament, depending on which kind each book is. The historical apocrypha will go with the historical Hebrew Books, the prophetical apocrypha will go with the prophetical Hebrew Books, and the Book of Sirach will go with the wisdom literature, or Writings.

Our Bibles today, then, have forty-seven books, not just the old Hebrew thirty-nine. For the Bible grew and grew as God's revelation to his people grew. In the time of the Babylonian Exile, in the 500s B.C., there were only five books, the books of the Torah. In the 400s, the six historical books were added. In the last two centuries B.C., just before Jesus, the Prophets, Writings, and Apocrypha were added.

God's Revelation, Christians feel, never stops. The number of the Books of the Bible had reached forty-seven by the time of Jesus. Then Christians added the twenty-seven books of the New Testament, as revelation took a great leap forward in Jesus, God's complete revelation, an actual person. Since then, the number of books in the Bible has not increased.

Jesus is God's complete revelation. Revelation is still growing, but it is growing as *we* grow, in our hearts and minds and in our world community—to the maturity and love and peace of Jesus, God's Revelation-in-Person.

3
The New Testament

As we have seen, the first part of the Bible, the longer part, is called the Old Testament. The second part, the shorter one—only about one-fourth of the whole Bible—is called the New Testament. A "testament," we saw, is a legal document that *testifies* that something has been done.

The Old Testament is the document that testifies that God and his people made a "covenant," a sacred contract. God guaranteed that he would be his people's God, and his people guaranteed that they would be his people. That is, God and the people of Israel guaranteed that they would always be faithful to each other. The Old Testament is the Jewish Bible.

Christians believe the Old Testament too. But Christians believe that Jesus is the Savior whom God in the Old Testament promised he would send one day. For, as we read in the Old Testament, while God was faithful to his people, his people were not faithful to him. They turned their backs on him by committing sins. So God promised that he would send them a Savior some day. And he promised he would make a New Covenant with them.

This is what the New Testament is all about. It is the document testifying that God and his people did, in fact, make a New Covenant, a new contract saying that he would be their God and they would be his people. But now, Christians say, God's people are not just the people of Israel, as in the Old Testament. Now, God wants *all* peoples as his people. Christians and Jews agree that God cannot fail to keep his promise to send a Savior. But Christians say he has already kept his promise, that the Savior is a Jewish man, a rabbi who lived in Palestine 2,000 years ago. His name is *Yeshuah* (yĕ-shōō-ĕ) which translates into English as "Jesus." "Yes," Christians say, "we have good news: God has sent us a Savior, and his name is Jesus." Jews say God has yet to send the Savior.

The Good News

This is why the first part of the New Testament is called the "Good News." It is the story of the life, death, and resurrection of the Savior, Jesus. "Good" in old English was spelled *god*. The word for "news," or "story," was *spel*. (Our modern word "spelling" comes from it, because when you tell a story you have to spell it out in words.) So "good news" in old English was *god spel*. And people talked about *this* good news so much that it became one word: "godspel." Finally, they dropped the *d* because it's hard to pronounce when you say it fast as one word. And our word "gospel" was born.

In Greek and Latin, too, the languages spoken by most of the first Christians, the gospel was called the good news. One of the words for "good" in Greek was *eu*. "News" was *angelion*. (This is why we call a messenger from God an "angel.") Now, if you put these two words together, you get the Greek word for "good news," or "gospel": *euangelion*. The Romans, who spoke Latin, changed it to *evangelium*, because the *u* was pronounced like a *v* anyway. This is why the traditional authors of the four Gospels (Matthew, Mark, Luke, and John) are called the four

"Evangelists." This is also why anything that has to do with the Gospels may be called "evangelical." Many Protestants, for instance, are called "evangelical Christians," or just "evangelicals," because they insist so strongly that Christians should go back in history behind their later traditions and learn Christianity from the Gospels themselves. Finally, this is why bringing the good news of the gospel to people is called "evangelization."

The Parts of the New Testament

The New Testament is in four parts. Not surprisingly, the first part is the four Gospels, since they are the story of Jesus.

But the Gospels are not the only writings in the New Testament. Just as the Old Testament may be divided into
1. The Law
2. The Prophets
3. The Writings
so the New Testament contains
1. The Gospels
2. The Acts of the Apostles
3. The Letters
4. The Book of Revelation
The Gospels make up about 40% of the New Testament. The Letters make up another 40%. That leaves about 20% for Acts and Revelation. Acts is about twice as long as Revelation.

The four Gospels are traditionally considered to be the writings of Saint Matthew, Saint Mark, Saint Luke, and Saint John, respectively. Like the rest of the New Testament, they were all written after Jesus' resurrection. The earliest Gospel (the second one in our bibles today, the Gospel According to Saint Mark) was written about A.D. 65, or about thirty-five years after Jesus' resurrection. The last Gospel to be written, the Gospel According to Saint John, was written in the A.D. 90s.

The Acts of the Apostles, a single book, is a continuation of the Gospel According to Luke, and was written in the middle A.D. 80s, not long after the Gospel According to Luke. It tells what happened to some of the first Christians, and what they did, after Jesus' resurrection.

Then come the Letters. They used to be called the "Epistles," which is another English word for "letters" and comes from the Greek *epi-,* "to" and *-stell-,* "send," because a letter is "sent to" someone. The traditional authors of the Letters of the New Testament are Saints Paul, John, Peter, James, and Jude. Some of Paul's letters were written only about twenty years after the resurrection, about A.D. 50. This makes them the oldest writings in the New Testament.

Some of the letters were addressed to individuals. For instance, Saint Paul wrote a letter to a person named Philemon, asking him to forgive a slave, Onesimus, for running away and even to set him free. But other letters were written to whole communities of new Christians, not just individuals.

The Book of Revelation, like the Fourth Gospel and three of the letters, was traditionally thought to have been written by the apostle Saint John. And indeed it probably was written by a member of a group of persons who followed the teaching of the apostle John. Revelation was written sometime around A.D. 90.

And that is the New Testament: the Gospels, the Acts of the Apostles, the Letters, and Revelation. It was all written during the first hundred years after Jesus' resurrection, the first one hundred years of the Christian Church.

Now let us look at the parts of the New Testament one by one.

The Four Gospels

On the first Pentecost Sunday, we are told, seven weeks after Jesus rose from the dead (*pentēk-ost* means "fifti-eth" in Greek, meaning here the fiftieth day of Jesus' new, risen life), the eleven apostles (the Twelve minus Judas) rushed from their hiding place, the Upper Room of the Last Supper. For weeks in there they had been trembling with fear of being caught and punished for being friends of the crucified Jesus. But then, with the fire of the Holy Spirit in their hearts, as it had been upon their heads when he had come in the form of wind and fire that morning, they ran out into the streets of Jerusalem to spread the good news everywhere: Jesus has risen from the dead!

So well did the apostles tell the story of Jesus' death and resurrection to all who would listen that in a few weeks there were thousands of Christians—followers of Jesus. Some of the new Christians were Jews, and some of them were "gentiles," meaning "foreigners," non-Jews; but all of them were on fire with the story of Jesus' death and resurrection.

And then the new Christians all wanted to know what Jesus had said and done *before* his death and resurrection. So they asked his friends the apostles. And the apostles told them. The apostles told the

new Christians how this rabbi named *Yeshuah*—
Jesus—had gone about all the countryside of
Galilee and Judea preaching the good news that the
Kingdom of God had finally come upon earth. And
they talked about how he had healed the sick and
forgiven sins. In other words, the apostles told the
new Christians all that Jesus had said and done that
showed he was the Savior, the one sent by God to
rescue his people from sin and suffering. And the
oral tradition of the Gospel was born. By word of
mouth, the mighty deeds of God were being
reported once more and recorded in people's mem-
ories, just as they had been in the Old Testament
generations before. Of course, there were no written Gospels as yet. The year was about A.D. 30, the
approximate year of Jesus' death and resurrection.
And this is the way things remained for the next
few years: Thousands of new Christians heard
about Jesus from those who had seen him, but
nothing was written down yet. One of the reasons
nothing was written down right away is that Jesus
had promised to come again some day, and people
thought that this would happen right away, perhaps
within just a few years.

As the years went by, however, people saw that
there would have to be a written record of the
things Jesus had said and done—His "words and
works." Some of the people who had seen Jesus
were growing older now, and some must have died.
So, about the middle of the first century, some of
the things the apostles had told the first Christians
about Jesus began to be written down. And the
written tradition of the Gospels was born.

By this time the apostles had given their eyewitness account of Jesus' words and works—his life, death, and resurrection—to thousands of people. And of course these people talked among themselves about what they had been told; and when still newer converts joined the Christians, they too were told all this. We know what happens, though, when stories are repeated from one person to another, and then to another. . . . The story is changed.

And so, many versions of the story of Jesus had begun to circulate by word of mouth. Naturally, then, when this oral tradition began to be transformed into written tradition, many different versions of the story of Jesus began to appear in writing.

There were dozens of "gospels" circulating in the first Christian communities, then, not just four. And each "reflected the oral tradition" that had produced it—that is, each was basically the same as a word-of-mouth account of Jesus' life, death, and resurrection that had been circulating among new Christians. But as we have seen, some of these oral accounts had become changed in the telling. And so, when the oral accounts were committed to writing, some of the writing, too, had departed from the apostles' first eyewitness accounts.

Some of these dozens of early "gospels," then, were a little strange, a little wild. Today we call these gospels "apocryphal," which, as we saw earlier, means "hidden," because the early Christians eventually "hid them away." That is, they pretty much forgot about them. And that is why not many of them were copied onto new scrolls when the old scrolls faded or crumbled, and why we do not have many of these "apocryphal gospels" today. "That's not the Jesus *I* know," we can imagine the first Christians saying. They felt they actually knew Jesus personally, even though they knew about him only by hearsay. When people told one another about Jesus, they did not discuss him the way you might explain to someone something out of your math book. They were so excited about him as a person that when they told about him, his personhood seemed to come through right with the story, and both the tellers and the hearers felt they knew and loved him personally. The first Christians did not think they needed any Scripture scholars to tell them which gospels were right and which were not. And so, over the years, this "primitive Christian community"—the very first Christians—began to ignore the apocryphal gospels, one by one. Some of these "gospels" are still extant today—that is, some of them are still around. We have already seen the story of the boy Jesus blessing his clay birds and causing them to fly away, so that he won the bird-making contest the children were having. But most of the apocryphal gospels have disappeared because the first Christians felt they weren't true. And only the four Gospels we have in our bibles today were accepted by all Christians.

The Authors of the Gospels

The four Gospels, then, were not physically written by the persons whose names are in their titles: Matthew, Mark, Luke, and John. Matthew and John were apostles, close friends of Jesus. Mark and Luke were close friends of the apostles. All four were completely involved in the *first* stage of the gospel tradition, the oral stage. They preached Jesus; they didn't write about him. Their stories of Jesus were written down, as we have seen, only after they had passed through the minds and hearts of a good many people.

Then why do the four Gospels bear the names of Matthew, Mark, Luke, and John, if Matthew, Mark, Luke, and John did not actually, physically write them? How did these writings come to be attributed to these four persons, as if they *had* actually written them?

The answer is, because the apostles *are* the "authors" of the Gospels, in a way. They are the "authors" of these four special little books in the *original* meaning of the word "author." Originally, "author" meant the person whose *ideas* were in a book, not the person who actually, physically wrote the ideas down. And of course the Gospels do report the *ideas* of the apostles. The Gospels do record the thoughts of these eyewitnesses of what Jesus said and did, because the Gospels came out of the oral tradition that goes back to the apostles' first excited stories about him.

Even today, when we see a book by "John Doe *with* Mary Jones," we know that John Doe may not have physically written a single line of the book. Most likely it was Mary Jones who penned, or typed, every word. But if the book publisher is honest, "John Doe with Mary Jones" means that Mary had many long conversations with John Doe before she wrote anything. She probably had her tape recorder going so she wouldn't forget anything John said. (The first Christians had no tape recorders, so they had to rely on their memory.) Mary Jones wrote the book from what she heard from John Doe, so that the ideas were his. So John is an author of the book too. In fact, he is the principal author, and Mary comes second.

It is somewhat like this with the Gospels "According to Matthew," "According to Mark," "According to Luke," and "According to John." Some other person, unknown to us today, actually penned each of our four Gospels. But he penned what he had heard from someone else, who had heard it from someone else, who had heard it from someone else . . . who had heard it from an apostle, who had actually seen Jesus doing and saying the things in the story.

Our titles are really not so bad after all, then. "According to Matthew" or "Mark" or "Luke" or "John" reminds us that it is Jesus' personal friends who are the "authors" of the Gospels in the original meaning of the word "author." It is they whose ideas about Jesus have come down to us in their Gospels.

Before we examine the Gospels individually we ought to notice one more thing—something we have seen before, when we were examining the Old Testament. The four Gospels we read today in our bibles are not the very first written versions, not the very first redactions, of those Gospels. As we have seen, in ancient days, as oral tradition passed into written form, it passed through several redactions before being set in final form. Just as had happened with the Old Testament, the New Testament, too, including the Gospels, was written, then edited, or adjusted a bit here and there, several times before being fixed in a final redaction—in the version we read in our bibles today. Here too, however, with the New Testament as with the Old, the community of believers watched hawk-like to see that no changes were made that would in any way falsify their faith-image of Jesus. And this is why Christians today, even educated Christians who know all about gospel "authorship," have faith in the Gospels just as if the Gospels had physically come from the hands and pens of Jesus' apostles.

Now it is time to look at some of the special characteristics of each of the four Gospels in turn. Here again, as in everything we can learn about the Bible and how it came to be, the work of the Scripture scholars is very important.

The Synoptic Gospels

One of the very first things a Scripture scholar notices about the four Gospels is that three of them are very much alike, while one is quite different. In fact, this is so clear that even an ordinary reader can see it. The three Gospels that are very much alike are the first three—the Gospels According to Matthew, Mark, and Luke. The one that tells Jesus' story in a different way is the Gospel According to John.

As a result, the first three Gospels are called the "Synoptic Gospels"—from the Greek *syn-*, "together," and *-optik-*, "viewed." The reason for the name is that if you were to snip the first three Gospels out of your bible and make one long column out of each one by laying the pages on the floor, for instance, so that you had three parallel columns, one for each of the first three Gospels, you could "see them together" (*syn-optik-*). You would see that they all go along pretty much the same in their structure. That is, they all three present pretty much the same events in Jesus' life and pretty much in the same order. In fact, you might notice that in many places they read exactly alike, word for word.

The Gospel According to Mark

The oldest Gospel—and the shortest—comes second among the Gospels as they appear in our bibles today. It is the **Gospel According to Mark.** It was written (in its final redaction, as we have it today) in the middle or late A.D. 60s, or about thirty-five years after Jesus' life on earth.

It was written to be read to gentiles. As we have seen, the very first Christians were almost all Jews. But within a few years after Jesus' resurrection, the new belief of these Jews had spread like wildfire among non-Jews as well; so then there were non-Jewish, or "gentile," Christians too. Some of these foreigners were people who had already been living in Palestine at the time of Jesus—Greek merchants, for example, who traded there, or Roman soldiers in the army of occupation; for Palestine, at the eastern end of the Mediterranean Sea, was part of the Roman Empire in the time of Jesus and the apostles. Then besides, the "good news" had spread beyond Palestine, too—to the actual homelands of these foreigners, or gentiles. And it was for them that the Gospel of Mark was written.

How do we know this? How do we know that the Gospel According to Mark was written to be read to gentiles? Mostly from internal evidence. Internal evidence, remember, is the evidence right in the text itself. (See page 24.) External evidence would be, for instance, what some *other* piece of writing might say about a Gospel, or some historical fact we know about from some other source that might tell us something about a Gospel.

On internal evidence alone, then—just from the words of the Gospel According to Mark—we can see quite readily that this little book must have been written for gentiles, who mostly spoke Greek. Scripture scholars have developed a whole network of proofs that it was. However, there is some internal evidence that even the beginner can appreciate, showing that Mark must have been written for gentile Christians. For example, Mark does not use the Hebrew word "Messiah," meaning the "Anointed One," the Savior whom God would "anoint" as a king and priest and send to his people. (This, incidentally, is the word Matthew uses.) Instead, he uses the Greek word for "Anointed One": "Christ." (In English, sacred ointments can be called "chrism.")

Like all the Gospels, the Gospel According to Mark was written in Greek. Mark's Greek is simple, straightforward—and really not very good Greek. It must have been written by an ordinary, not extremely well-educated person. And as we might expect, it was popular especially among ordinary people, who loved to hear it because it "talked their language." Below, we shall see that all the Gospels were written mainly to be read to the people as part of their celebration of the Lord's Supper, the Eucharist. So of course people did not need to be able to read in order to appreciate the Gospel According to Mark, any more than they had to in order to appreciate any of the other Gospels.

The fact that the oldest Gospel, the Gospel According to Mark, was written only about thirty-five years after Jesus' resurrection must not, of course, lead us to the conclusion that it was the first thing to be written about the life of Jesus. No, it is only the "final redaction" of a whole series of writings—whether many or few we are not sure—and these redactions or versions must have been copied at least partly from still other writings. And those writings in turn came out of the oral tradition that goes back to the apostles and that exciting day of the first Pentecost when Jesus' friends were filled with the Holy Spirit and tumbled out onto the streets of Jerusalem to tell the world the good news of Jesus.

But the earlier writings, from which our final redaction of Mark, the one we read today, was taken, were soon lost. The Gospel of Mark—along with our other three Gospels, of course—seemed so true, and filled their early Christian hearers with such faith, that Christian people no longer felt a need to hear any earlier writings; so that as a result, these earlier writings about Jesus' life, death, and resurrection were no longer copied, and they crumbled to dust. But the Gospel According to Mark was copied and copied by hand, then canonized—that is, fixed in a canon, or official list of sacred writings—then copied and copied some more down through the centuries, until the invention of the printing press. (In the days before the printing press and good, sturdy paper, canonization was the only sure way for a sacred writing to survive at all!)

Another particularly interesting and important thing about the Gospel According to Mark is that both of the other Synoptic Gospels—Matthew and Luke, the first and third Gospels in our bibles— "depend" on Mark. That is, one of the documents the writers of Matthew and Luke used when they were writing their own Gospels was the Gospel of Mark, which had already been written and circulated.

This is easy to prove from internal evidence. Perhaps the most striking piece of internal evidence is that more than ninety percent of the Gospel of Mark simply is repeated, often word for word, in the Gospel of Matthew! Likewise, over half of Mark appears in Luke. The Gospel According to Mark was a very important Gospel indeed for the first Christians.

One of the most interesting and exciting things about the Gospel According to Mark is its insistence on what we today call the "Messianic secret"—the Messiah's secret, Jesus' secret, something he knew about the Messiah that he did not want people to tell.

And what was Jesus' secret?

For a long time it was thought that it was only that Jesus was the Messiah. But recent scholarship has shown that this was only *part* of the secret Jesus tells his followers not to reveal. The *whole* secret was this: that the last shall be first in the Kingdom of God— that the poor and the lowly are God's favorite persons. And then *part* of this secret was another scandalous piece of information: that the poor and lowly Jesus—the last person to be thought of as important by the corrupt and selfish elements in the religion and government of his day—was really first of all in the eyes of God; in fact he was the Savior, the Christ, sent from God to heal his people. And the rest of the secret was that this Savior, this Chosen One of God, the Promised One of Israel, was to suffer and die. Everyone had thought the Savior would have to be great, and be a king—everyone, that is, who had not read the Old Testament prophecies about the Suffering Servant in the Book of Isaiah.

Once this secret finally got out—after Jesus' death

and resurrection—it came as a great shock to the established powers, because it revolutionized religion. In the eyes of the first Christians, Jesus' resurrection was living proof that the poor and the lowly, the outcast and despised, were really God's favorite people. Jesus had been tortured to death like a slave on the cross, but then he had risen and would be king of the world some day.

A great part of the interest of reading the Gospels, then, expecially Mark, is reading the first Christians' completely new and "upside-down" religion, the first Christians' "backwards idea" of who is important to God: the helpless, the suffering—the "little ones" of the earth.

Now it is even easier to see why simple, poor, uneducated people loved to call Mark's message a "gospel." It surely came as good news to the lowly. Of course, the same is also true of the other Gospels, for the "Messianic secret" is featured in the others, too, even if it is not always as plain as it is in Mark.

Another very important characteristic of the Gospel of Mark is its emphasis on Jesus' suffering, his martyrdom. Nearly half of this book, the shortest of all the Gospels, is devoted to the story of Jesus' passion (from the Latin *passio,* "suffering") and death.

But the main point of the Gospel According to Mark—and, as we shall see, this is the main point of the other Gospels, too—regarding behavior, is that Jesus promised to come back again. And so Christians are supposed to behave in such a way as to have his kingdom ready for him when he returns—a kingdom of love and peace.

The Gospel According to Matthew

The second oldest Gospel is the **Gospel According to Matthew.** This Gospel appears first in our bibles, and whereas Mark is the shortest gospel, Matthew is the longest. Matthew is more than one-and-one-half times as long as Mark. It was written in Greek sometime in the A.D. 70s.

The Gospel According to Matthew was written for Jewish Christian audiences. As we have seen, Matthew uses the Hebrew related word, *Messiah,* for "Anointed One" in speaking of Jesus, while Mark uses the gentile word *Christ,* a Greek word, to mean the same thing. Another difference between Matthew and Mark is that Matthew makes a number of remarks about Old Testament prophecies, which he says Jesus fulfilled. Whatever the Old Testament said about the Savior who was to come, Matthew teaches, Jesus fits the description perfectly. Mark, on the other hand, does not seem to have much interest in stressing the Old Testament prophecies. Here again, then, is solid internal evidence that Matthew was written for Jews, while Mark was written for gentiles, or non-Jews, who did not know the Old Testament very well anyway.

Of course, both Gospels were written for Christians. When we say Jews or gentiles here, we mean Jewish Christians and gentile Christians. It may sound strange to us today to hear of Jewish Christians, but as we have seen, the very first Christians were largely Jews. After all, Jews and Christians believed almost all the same things. Both groups believed that God had promised to send a Savior, and that God never lies. The only difference is that the Christian Jews believed that the Savior had come, and was Jesus, while the non-Christian Jews believed that the Savior had not yet come, and would be someone else.

So if we think about it, it is not so surprising that the first Christians were Jews. After all, Jesus was a Jew and a rabbi. The apostles, his closest followers, were all Jews. And all his life long, he never stepped outside of the little country of Palestine, the country of the Jews. When the apostles rushed into the streets of Jerusalem to tell the world Jesus had risen from the dead, most of the first people they preached to were Jews, though there were also some foreigners, some gentiles, in the crowds. And so naturally the first converts to the infant religion—the "Christians," as they would soon be called—were Jews. But these Jewish converts *to* Christianity were not converts *from* Judaism. They remained members of the Jewish faith. Like all Jews, they lived for the day the Savior would come. The only difference was that Christian Jews believed that day *had* come.

Even after the Church spread out beyond Palestine and began to include more and more gentiles—all the way from Spain in the West to India in the East, so that there were actually more gentile Christians than Jewish Christians—Jewish Christian communities continued to exist. But sadly, gentile Christians persecuted them because they were Jews (even though they were Christians too) and eventually destroyed these communities. They lasted only into the A.D. 400s (in Spain, till around A.D. 900).

And so the Gospel According to Mark was written to be read to gentile Christians. The Gospel According to Matthew was written to be read to Jewish Christians. But as we have seen, Matthew "depends" on Mark. That is, one of the books the writer of Matthew used was the Gospel According to Mark. In fact, as we have seen, the writer of Matthew simply copied all of Mark into Matthew (until he had almost two-thirds of his Gospel written in this fashion). But then he turned to other sources for the remainder of his Gospel (the one-third that is not the same as Mark). What were these sources?

Besides copying from Mark, the writer of Matthew also copied from the famous lost book of the logia of

54

Jesus. *Logia* is an old Greek word for "sayings." In the days of the first Christians, there seems to have been a book of Jesus' sayings, which was probably quite popular. Today that book has been lost. It was not a Gospel; it was probably not even an apocryphal gospel, one of the many "gospels" the first Christians eventually forgot about. No, it was not the story of Jesus' life, death, and resurrection at all, it would seem. Perhaps this is why it did not survive. It was only a book of his sayings, perhaps. And today it is lost because it did not continue to be copied from scroll to scroll down through the centuries. But the logia themselves, the sayings of Jesus, did not all disappear. The writer of the Gospel According to Matthew took some of them and interwove them with the material he was copying from the Gospel According to Mark.

And so, besides the Gospel of Mark, the most important book used by the writer of Matthew was the book of the logia, the lost book of the sayings of Jesus.

Then the writer of Matthew must have used some other sources besides, because there are a few things in Matthew that are not in Mark and that are not sayings of Jesus. These things too were probably taken from some written source, although it is just possible that the writer of Matthew took them directly from oral tradition. Scripture scholars are always making new discoveries in their science, and we still have many things to learn about the Bible, things that no one knows yet!

Matthew's picture of Jesus, then, is much fuller than the blunt, plain-talk picture in Mark. Matthew is warmer and more passionate. All the Gospels, as we have seen, were written mainly to be read in the celebration of the Lord's Supper, the Eucharist. When Christians came together on Saturday evenings to dine together and then celebrate the Eucharist, naturally they spent most or much of their meal talking with one another about Jesus, whose resurrection had taken place on a Sunday morning. But as the Christian community grew larger and larger and spread farther and farther out from Jerusalem, where the apostles had done their first preaching, fewer people were present that had actually heard the apostles talk about him. So people celebrating the Eucharist called for something in writing, something that someone who could read would read to them during their joyous suppers, something about Jesus' words and works. This is how the Gospels came to be, and this is what they were used for.

But the favorite was the Gospel According to Matthew: it was the most exciting. In fact, the first Christians' picture of Jesus was mostly made of the stories in Matthew. The word "church" is used in the Gospels only in Matthew. "Church," as we shall see, means the Christian community. Only the Gospel of Matthew talks about how the Church ought to behave, the things it ought to do to be really the Church of Jesus. So the first Christians especially loved to listen to the Gospel of Matthew at the Eucharist.

But of all the special things in Matthew, the most special are the five long sermons of Jesus that it contains—making Matthew perfect for reading at the Eucharist, of course. Christians thought that they could scarcely invite a better preacher than Jesus himself.

The Gospel According to Luke

The **Gospel According to Luke** was written in Greek, like all the others. But this time it was in good Greek, "literary" Greek. Obviously it was written by a more educated person and with a more educated audience in mind. Like Matthew, it "depends" on Mark—the Gospel According to Luke was written partly by copying what was already in the Gospel According to Mark.

Obviously the writer of Luke, like the writer of Matthew before him, thought much of Mark too precious not to copy and pass on. (After all, all the Gospels were written for the needs of different groups, and if no one had copied anything from the others, only one group would have heard that particular thing—Christian Jews, or uneducated Christian gentiles, or educated Christian gentiles.) But while Matthew copies almost all of Mark, Luke copies only about half.

Like Matthew, Luke too uses the book of the logia, the lost book of the sayings of Jesus.

Finally, again like Matthew, Luke adds material of its own to what Mark and the book of logia have to say. Luke, like Matthew, adds material taken from other lost writings about Jesus. The writer of Luke worked about A.D. 80.

Perhaps here would be a good place to summarize the main things we know about the sources of the Synoptic Gospels. Mark's written sources are unknown to us, although we know there must have been earlier redactions than the one in our bibles. But Matthew and Luke both used (1) Mark, (2) the lost book of logia, and (3) special written material that each one had but that the other did not have or did not choose to use.

Perhaps the most special thing about Luke's Gospel is that it stresses the humanness of Jesus. It emphasizes Jesus as a human being. Matthew, as we have seen, emphasizes Jesus' Messiahship, his Saviorhood, his fulfillment of the Old Testament prophecies. And John, as we shall see, emphasizes his Godhood. But Luke is specially careful to show us that Jesus prays to God, that he is loyal to the will of God his Father, even though it may be hard for him. Jesus is very human.

Another special thing about Luke is its insistence that the *anawim* (ä-nä-wĭm), the poor, the lowly, the people that others considered outcasts, are actually

God's favorite people. This reminds us of Mark's emphasis on the Messianic secret—the "topsy-turvy of the gospel," according to which the last shall be first, for God's ways are not our ways. And so too, in Luke, it is mainly for the *anawim,* the despised people of the earth, that the Savior has come.

The Fourth Gospel

The first three Gospels, the Synoptic Gospels, are very much alike, then. They can be "seen together," running parallel to one another and saying very much the same things about the life, death, and resurrection of Jesus.

The **Fourth Gospel,** however, is a very different kind of report. In the Synoptics, Jesus is pictured as a human being, although we do catch a glimpse of the divine about him from time to time. In the Fourth Gospel, things are just the other way around: Jesus is portrayed as God and the Son of God although we do catch a glimpse of his humanness from time to time. This is the main difference between the Fourth Gospel and the Synoptic Gospels.

But there are other differences as well, and very important ones. For instance, the events and sayings that the writer of John selects for recording in his Gospel are not usually the same events that the Synoptic writers think are most important. For, again, the writer of the Fourth Gospel is more interested in Jesus' glory and his godhood, and so the events and sayings he selects are the ones that best reflect that glory and that godhood. Even the cross, in this Gospel, is Jesus' glory, when he is "lifted up from earth" so that he can "draw all men to himself." And we can almost see him, a king on a throne, with his arms reaching out to embrace us all. Jesus is the human God, "God become man," who willingly took our sin and suffering on himself, so that we would not sin or have to suffer again.

The Fourth Gospel was written in Greek in the A.D. 90s. By this time the Church was already more gentile than it was Jew, and the Gospel According to John was written for a gentile audience.

One of the outstanding features of the Gospel of John is its inspiring accounts of Jesus' seven great miracles—from changing water to wine at the wedding in Cana to raising his friend Lazarus from the dead. Truly this person is the Son of God, says John, and he will never let us forget this even for an instant. The Kingdom of God is among us at last, and we do not have to wait for Jesus to "come again" to have him as our king. In the Synoptics, by contrast, all the emphasis is on the moment when he will come again to take final possession of his Kingdom.

The Acts of the Apostles

Now we have seen the Gospels—the story of the life, death, and resurrection of the Savior whom God has sent to snatch us from the jaws of death and restore us to everlasting life.

But then what happened? What happened *after* Jesus' resurrection, *after* his return to his Father in heaven, to come again some day? The Gospels end when Jesus, risen from the dead, ascends to his Father, to be seated at his right hand in the kingdom of the skies. His kingdom on earth (except perhaps in John) will have to wait. What about his friends, who are left here on earth?

This is where the fifth Book of the New Testament, the **Acts of the Apostles,** takes over. As its name suggests, this book recounts the words and actions of some of the apostles after Jesus had left them.

Not surprisingly, then, Acts begins with Pentecost Sunday, the day the apostles so excitedly began to preach the Gospel, the Good News, and the day on which the Christian community was born. Acts is the story of the infancy of the Christian Church.

The writer of the Gospel According to Luke also wrote the Acts of the Apostles, in Greek, sometime in the middle of the A.D. 80s, not long after writing the Gospel of Luke itself.

The writer of Acts meant Luke and Acts to be read together, in tandem. Acts continues explaining, to a relatively well-educated gentile audience, that the new religion of Jesus was meant for everyone, not just the Jews. It tells how the apostles preached first to Jews, then to gentiles in Palestine, then to gentile audiences outside Palestine, farther and farther westward into the Roman Empire, until they actually reached Rome, half the length of the Mediterranean away. In fact, one of the apostles, Saint Paul, went all the way to Spain at the western end of the great sea.

While Christianity was spreading westward from Palestine, toward Italy and Spain, it was also spreading north to Syria and south to Egypt. But Acts was written for the Christians of the West, and so it tells us only about the West.

According to Acts, you do not have to be a Jew to be a Christian. Many people assumed you did. After all, Christianity had been started by a Jew, Jesus; it had been started among Jews; and it had started as a variation on Jewish religion: *all* Jews believed God's promise to send a Messiah, a Savior, and *these* Jews believed the Messiah had already come and believed they knew who he was. So naturally, one might think you had to be a Jew to be a Christian. And the first gentile converts to Christianity actually had become *both* Jews *and* Christians. But no, says Acts, you can be a gentile Christian.

And so it has been ever since, down through the Christian centuries. You no longer have to be a Jew to be a Christian. In fact, most Christians have been gentiles.

The Letters of the New Testament

After the four Gospels—Matthew, Mark, Luke, and John—and the fifth Book of the New Testament, the Acts of the Apostles, come the "Letters of the Apostles." At least this is the order in which they appear in our bibles. As we shall see, however, some of these letters are the earliest writings in the New Testament.

The letters were written in Greek and, like the Gospels, make up about forty percent of the New Testament.

The Letters of Saint Paul

When we come to the letters, we finally know exactly who wrote some of the books of the New Testament: Some of them were written by Saint Paul, called "the Apostle."

There are twenty-one letters in the New Testament. Of these, thirteen are entitled **"Letter of Paul."** And of these thirteen, which the ancient title-writers thought were all by Paul, the following actually were written by Paul:

1. The Letter to the Romans
2. The First Letter to the Corinthians
3. The Second Letter to the Corinthians
4. The Letter to the Galatians
5. The Letter to the Philippians
6. The First Letter to the Thessalonians
7. The Letter to Philemon

Paul was not one of Jesus' twelve apostles. Then why is he called "the Apostle," as if he were *the* Apostle, the greatest of the apostles? (Actually he calls himself "the least of the apostles.")

Ancient Christian tradition said: To be an apostle—from the Greek *apo-*, "away," or "out," and *-stell-*, "send"—you must have been "sent out" by *Jesus personally,* to carry his message to others. And Saint Paul seems to have traveled farther, and preached to more groups of people, than any other of the earliest Christian missionaries. Therefore, in the minds of the early Christians, he came to be *the* Apostle.

But if Saint Paul was not one of the twelve apostles, whom Jesus had appointed during his lifetime on earth, and if indeed Paul had never even laid eyes on Jesus during his lifetime on earth, then how can Jesus have "sent him out" to be an apostle?

According to the Acts of the Apostles, Paul *did* see Jesus, and Jesus *did* send him forth to preach his good news. According to Acts, a certain person named Saul, a vicious persecutor of Christians, was on his way to arrest some more Christians one day, when suddenly he was thrown from his horse by a brilliant vision that struck him like a lightning bolt and blinded him. Lying helpless on the ground, he had to be helped up and taken into the city, where he told one and all of the vision he had seen. He had seen Jesus, he said, Jesus in the flesh, risen and glorious; and this Jesus had identified himself: "I am Jesus, whom you are persecuting!" So when you persecute a Christian you are persecuting Jesus, Paul learned! And later he developed this notion into the idea of the Body of Christ alive today, of which Jesus is the head and Christians are his arms and legs, his "members," doing the things he wants done on earth and taking care of one another the way one hand takes care of the other. This event is known throughout Christian history as the "Conversion of Saint

Paul"—for Saul then changed his name to "Paul" (a name which could not help but suggest "the little one" to people who understood Latin) and claimed to be the least of the apostles. For, he said, he had seen Jesus alive—in his vision—and Jesus had "sent him forth" to preach his good news. And then the "least of the apostles" became so busy in the service of the new faith that he has gone down in Christian history as *the* Apostle. Like his great friend Saint Peter, whom he both argued with and worked for, Saint Paul suffered a martyr's death in Rome, sometime in the A.D. 60s.

And it is this Paul who has written seven of the letters of the New Testament.

If we review the dates we have given for the first five books of the New Testament—the four Gospels and Acts—we see that these dates all fall between A.D. 60 and 100. Now if we compare this time-span with the date of Paul's death in Rome in the A.D. 60s, we shall at once suspect that Paul's letters may be among the earliest writings in the New Testament.

And our suspicions are confirmed. As a matter of fact, the Letters of Paul were written before anything else in the New Testament—before the Gospels, before Acts, and before the Book of Revelation. The reason the Gospels and Acts appear ahead of the letters in our bibles is that the Gospels are the story of Jesus and Acts is the sequel to, the continuation of, the third Gospel; and Jesus himself, of course, is the central message of the New Testament. So Christians listed the Gospel scrolls and Acts before the letters when they made up their official lists, their canons, of the New Testament.

To whom is Saint Paul writing these letters? Why is he writing them? Why are they in the Bible?

Of his seven letters, six are addressed to whole

Christian communities. The seventh is to an individual, Philemon. Paul was an extremely forceful, magnetic personality, and he had a powerful way of saying things. His letters so gripped and inspired the people who received them that they told everyone about them and passed them from hand to hand. Paul's letters became famous. By A.D. 100 they had been copied and recopied many times, collected on scrolls, and sent to Christian communities all over the eastern Mediterranean basin. When these Christian communities read them, they too found them gripping and inspiring; and surely they were true and important, they thought, so they read them at the Eucharist, right along with the Gospels and Acts. As a result, when the Christian people came to draw up their canons of the New Testament—their lists of the documents that set forth God's new sacred Covenant with his new people, their lists of what books told the whole truth about Jesus and ought to be read at the Supper they celebrated each week in his memory— they naturally included the Letters of Paul right along with the Gospels and Acts. At least by the year A.D. 100, or about thirty years after his martyrdom, copies of Paul's collected letters were read all over the Mediterranean Christian world.

As a matter of fact, Paul himself obviously intended his letters to be read aloud to the church, the Christian community, to whom they were addressed. This is evident from the internal evidence of his style of writing, his way of saying things. He probably did not know that after his death these seven letters would be read not only by the particular Christian communities to which they were addressed, but to Christian communities all over that part of the world. Knowing Paul, though, we can be pretty sure he would have been glad of it, because if there was ever a Christian on fire for Jesus and sure that his own ideas about Jesus were right, it was Paul, the Apostle.

When we say that Paul intended his letters to be read aloud in the church to which they were addressed, we do not mean they were intended to be read aloud in a church *building*. There were no church buildings in those days. The original meaning of the word "church" is: community of God's people. A "church," then, in the original meaning of the word, is a group of Christians who worship God together. (Even today, we still speak of the "local church." For instance, we say that a bishop is the head of the local church. We mean that he is the head of the Christians of this particular city, the Christian community in this locality.) But Christians did not worship in a special building devoted to that purpose. Not at first. Christians met in one another's homes to celebrate the Eucharist. They saw no need of a special, sacred place in which to meet to celebrate the Eucharist. Just celebrating the Eucharist, the supper they ate in memory of Jesus' death and resurrection as they waited for him to come again, was sacred enough, even if it happened to be in somebody's house. This is what would happen: Christians would gather for a meal together, a supper, once a week. They called their supper a "love feast," because they remembered what Jesus had said to the apostles on the night before he died: "This is how all will know you for my disciples: your love for one another" (John 13:35). That was the same night on which he had taken supper with the very first Christians, the apostles, and had broken bread for them to eat, saying that it was his body being broken for them. And he had poured out wine for them to drink, saying it was his blood being poured out for them; and he had asked them to continue to do this after he was gone. And so they did, and so they always have. And so they also referred to their supper as a "Eucharist," meaning a thanksgiving, because they were grateful for Jesus.

They would gather for a supper and pray and sing and talk. And they would listen to readings—part of a Letter of Paul, for instance, and then part of one of the Gospels. Then, as dawn approached—the dawn light in which their friend Jesus had risen from the dead one Sunday morning several years before, they would celebrate their Eucharist: They would break bread as his body, and pour out wine as his blood, and share that with one another too, as they had shared the other food of their "love feast."

And all of this happened in the dining room of somebody's house. But this was possible only because the communities of Christians were small. As more and more people became Christians—for Christian faith and enthusiasm was catching!—more and more room was needed to celebrate the Eucharist. Finally only the rich had room enough in their homes to invite all the Christians in town to the Eucharist. But even then there were no church *buildings*. In fact, to have had church buildings could have been very dangerous at times: the Roman Empire often sought out and punished Jews and Christians, because Jews and Christians refused to worship the emperor as a god. Jews and Christians claimed to have a commandment, given them by some strange god somebody named Moses had met in the Sinai peninsula one night: "You shall have no other gods before me." To refuse to worship the emperor was punishable by law. So the Eucharist often had to be held in secret in the days of the first Christians.

Much later, in A.D. 312, the Roman emperor Constantine legalized the Christian religion. Suddenly no one's home, not even the richest Christian's home, was large enough to hold the whole Christian community of a town. Sometimes that meant practically everyone in town! Once Christianity was legal, it spread even faster. So church buildings began to be built, just one in a town at first, since Christians always considered it important to pray together and to do as many things as possible together. They wanted to stay *united* in love and in the worship of God as they gathered around the eucharistic memorial of their great friend.

It is certainly easy to see why Paul's letters, like the other letters and especially like the Gospels, became so important. *The whole New Testament was written to be read in church communities at the Eucharist.* And as Christians multiplied and celebrations of the Eucharist grew more crowded, the writings of the New Testament were heard by more and more people. Soon Paul's name was on everyone's lips, just as the name of Jesus was.

Then something happened. In some places, people became so enthusiastic about Paul and his teaching that when asked what religious community they belonged to they would answer, "the church of Paul" instead of "the Church of Jesus"! Paul heard about it and did not like it. He wrote a letter in which he said that no matter who converted them, it was really Jesus by whose grace they were believers and Jesus to whom they belonged—Jesus alone. This letter, too, was read in all the churches, the first Christian communities, and it helped Christians to feel a "sacred togetherness" even among different communities. They felt their oneness across the miles. They felt that they were one Church—one Christian community, worldwide, tied together by the bond of all belonging to Jesus, even when they did not physically worship God together. The churches were one Church.

In Hebrew, "church" is *qahal*. In Greek it is *ekklēsia*. In Latin it is *ecclesia*. And all three words mean the same: the community of those "called apart," "called aside," to belong in a special way to God. (*Ek-* or *ex-* in Greek means "out," or "apart," and *-klē-* means "called.") This is what "church" means in English today, in its first meaning: the community of the people of God.

It is easy to see what a help it must have been to have the same Gospels and the same Letters read in all the churches of the early Christian world. People were helped to be "one" in love and service to their friend Jesus and to one another, no matter how different they were from one another otherwise—Jew and Greek, slave and free, rich and poor.

Paul did not write his letters with his own hand. He dictated them to a companion, a man who acted as his secretary. Sometimes he traveled with one companion, sometimes with another, so he had many secretaries. But after he had dictated a letter, he almost always took the quill from his secretary and added a few words in his own hand; and you can read what he put down right at the end of nearly any of his seven letters.

The Other Letters

We do not know the exact identity of the writers of the **other fourteen letters** of the New Testament—the ones not written by Paul. The name of Paul, Peter, John, James, or Jude appears in their titles, but the person who actually did the writing was someone else in each case. In ancient times, it was the custom for a writer to put a famous person's name on the thing he was writing, if he simply wanted to get his message across and be believed, not to become famous himself. He did this especially if he thought that what he was writing *could have* been written by the famous person whose name he was using, if only he had thought of it! Thus, for example, the three letters called the First, Second, and Third Letters of John were not actually written by the apostle Saint John, and the Second and Third were not written by whoever wrote the Fourth Gospel. Still, all three letters are so much like the Fourth Gospel in what they say and how they say it, that these letters must have all been written by the same *group* of persons, who were perhaps disciples of disciples of the apostle John, that is, followers of his followers.

As we have seen, Paul's letters were written in the A.D. 50s and 60s and were read in all the churches at the Eucharist by the year A.D. 100, or perhaps a little earlier. The other letters were not written this early, nor were they accepted by all the churches so promptly. Of the twenty-one letters of the New Testament, the fourteen Paul did not write were written only in the last part of the first century A.D.; and some were generally accepted by all the churches only in the middle of the A.D. 300s! The letters that had to wait *this* long to be accepted are five of the last seven in our bibles—the *Letters* attributed to *Peter, John, James, and Jude* (all except the First Letter of Peter and the First Letter of John, which did not have to wait so long to be accepted).

The Christian people were extremely careful about which letters they thought told the truth about Jesus and which did not! After all, these letters were going to be read to them in their celebration of their memorial suppers in honor of Jesus.

These last seven letters in our bibles—the ones with the names of Peter, John, James, and Jude in their titles—are called the "Catholic Letters."

"Catholic" mans "universal," and the word "catholic" as used in describing the last seven letters of the New Testament did not at first refer to the "Catholic Church" in the modern sense. It meant that these letters were addressed to the universal Church, the whole Christian Church, all the local churches at once, and not just to one church, one Christian community, as Paul's letters had been. The Catholic Letters are very interesting to us today if we wish to learn how the first Christians lived and prayed and what their worries and problems were.

The Book of Revelation

The last book of the New Testament—and therefore the last book of the Bible—is the **Book of Revelation.** It was written about A.D. 90. Like the rest of the New Testament, it was written in Greek. Like the Fourth Gospel and the Catholic Letters of John, it was written by someone who studied and prayed in a group of Christians which had been formed by followers of the apostle Saint John, the "disciple Jesus loved" so much.

The Book of Revelation is a Book of apocalypse— wild visions, cataclysms, catastrophes, warnings, prophecies, and judgments. The new little Christian Church was suffering cruel persecution in A.D. 90. Sometimes Jews and Christians were persecuted and even killed just for being Jews or Christians, even if they could not be convicted of the crimes they were accused of. Christians, for instance, were sometimes accused of sacrificing infants and devouring their flesh. Christians, we know, often had to celebrate their Eucharist in secret, for fear of being all caught together in one place; and of course they did believe that the bread they broke and the wine they poured out was Somebody's flesh and blood. They believed it was the flesh and blood of Jesus. But by the time the story reached the ears of the Roman secret police it had become the flesh and blood of babies. Even today we know that when people seem different from us we are tempted to call them strange just because they are strangers, and sometimes we believe the most outlandish, improbable things about them. This is what often happened to Jews and Christians in the Roman Empire long ago. The Romans, whose gods were a plain, reasonable sort, like Jupiter or Diana or the reigning emperor, all with head and arms and legs and hands and feet like anybody else, thought these little people from the Middle East most strange, with their tale of a god who was invisible. But the tale told that this god had had a child, a son, who had come to earth and walked and worked in Palestine—then had died and come back to life again! And later, it appeared, these strange people from the East began to have secret feasts at night, in which this son of the god miraculously took part! Then when the Romans found out that this Palestinian Jew, the supposed son of the strange, invisible, oriental god, was the grand and glorious "King of Heaven" whom these funny Jews prayed to—well, this was just too much! The Romans had heard that he was some obscure little trouble-maker who had tried to get himself made king of the Jews and had ended up dying the torture-death reserved for slaves—hanging nailed to crossed boards, till he died of suffocation from his own weight. So if these strange people were accused of eating babies, this was no longer much of a surprise. People like that would probably do anything. So Christians, like Jews, were often cruelly persecuted by the Roman Empire.

This is what the last book of the Bible, the Book of

Revelation, is all about: the Roman persecutions, and how God would punish the persecutors and reward the victims—provided they had been faithful to the death.

But the story of the persecutions and punishments and rewards is not told straight out in simple narrative form. The Book of Revelation tells its story in highly picturesque, symbolic form. In one vision, for instance, a woman is in childbirth, while a terrible dragon waits at her feet to devour the offspring as soon as it is born. In another, four horsemen come thundering down on the world and threaten to destroy it.

The story of the persecution is the story of the world, Revelation says. Good and evil are locked in a battle to the death. And good shall triumph, because nobody is stronger than God, but not before tremendous explosions of love and hate have rocked the earth to its foundations.

4
From Quill to Printing Press: The World's Best-Seller

In our first three chapters we have seen (1) how the Bible came to be, (2) the Old Testament and its parts, and (3) the New Testament and its parts. Now it is time to see how the Bible has come down to us who live two thousand years after it was written.

No other book in the history of the world has been as popular as the Bible. For three thousand years—while it was being written, and ever since—millions of people have read it, studied it, prayed it, and lived their lives by it. It is easy to see why millions of copies have been necessary. And so we are not surprised to learn that, even back in the days of papyrus, parchment, quill, and brush, the books of the Bible were the most-copied manuscripts of all time. Then later, when the invention of the printing press made book production hundreds of times easier and faster than ever before, the book most printed was—and still is—the Bible. In fact, the very first book to be printed, in the A.D. 1400s, was the Bible.

It will be interesting, then, to look at this process of "transmission"—how the Bible got from its authors and the first believing communities to us today. We have already seen how the Bible originally came to be. We saw in Chapter 1 how the process of oral tradition finally began to be crystallized—redacted several times, then fixed, or put through its final redaction, ready to be transmitted from the first manuscript to us, down through two thousand years of copying and printing.

So now we shall look at some of the interesting things that have happened to the Bible in the process of being copied by hand (until the A.D. 1400s) and then printed (after the A.D. 1400s).

Of course, one of the most important things that happened to the Bible during these nineteen centuries was that it was translated. If all the manuscripts of the Bible had been *only* copied, we would just have to say, "It's all Greek (or Hebrew) to me!" and most of us would not be able to read a single word. But fortunately for people who do not read ancient Hebrew and ancient Greek, the Bible has been translated into—you guessed it—hundreds of languages, all over the globe, as we might expect of the best-seller of all time.

Let's look, then, at the three things that happened to the Bible after its oral tradition finally got into writing more than two thousand years ago. The Bible was (1) copied by hand, (2) translated, and (3) printed.

Manuscripts—"Written by Hand"

The word "manuscript" actually means "hand written." As we have seen, before the invention of printing, as more copies of any scroll of the Bible were needed or as the old copies became too tattered to use, new copies had to be made. The new copies were made in the same way as the old ones—by copying the words from the old scroll onto the new, word by word and letter by letter, with a quill (called a "pen," from the Latin *penna,* or "feather") or a brush.

The letters were usually penned onto the papyrus

or parchment in either of two styles. If they were capital letters they were called "uncials," from the Latin word for "inch," the last knuckle of the thumb used as a measuring stick. If they were small letters they were called "minuscules" (from *minus,* the Latin word for "smaller," or "less") and were written in "cursive" (or "running") form—with curves instead of corners, just as we do in longhand today.

As we have seen, all this copying by hand down through the centuries occasionally led to changes and errors in the words. For example, sometimes a copyist might skip a line and not even notice it. Or sometimes he might do just the opposite and copy the same thing twice. Of course, most such errors could be easily corrected the next time that manuscript was copied. The new copyist could usually see the mistake and fix it almost automatically. In fact, the people who used the manuscript in the meantime would write in the correct words between the lines or in the margin when they saw an error, and then when the manuscript came to be copied, the copyist would have an even easier time correcting the error.

This led copyists to try to recognize errors and correct them. Sometimes, then, a copyist would find what he thought was a previous copyist's mistake when it really wasn't a mistake, and change it to what he thought was right.

But there are "families of manuscripts," that is, those copied from manuscripts copied from other manuscripts, and so on, back into history, like a family tree. Often the manuscripts in the same family tree contained the same error, then. As we have seen, it is the task of Scripture scholars to sort out the errors by comparing manuscripts with one another and restoring the correct wording. And they do an excellent job of it. Our bibles today are much more accurate than the old manuscripts were.

Here is a particularly interesting example of a change that crept into the Bible because of something one copyist did. Why does the Lord's Prayer, the Our Father, sometimes end, ". . . for Thine is the kingdom, and the power, and the glory," and sometimes not?

To answer this question, we must first point out that the old copyists often used the margins of their scrolls for two things: (1) When they noticed that they had skipped something, sometimes they wrote it in the margin, so that the next copyist would see it and put it in correctly; and (2) when they had copied something particularly difficult to understand, or particularly inspiring, they might write a little explanation or some expression of joy or reverence, in the margin. (A marginal note is called a "gloss," from the Greek *glott-,* or *gloss-,* meaning "tongue," or "word," meaning a difficult word being explained).

Well, it would appear that one day a copyist was copying the Gospel According to Matthew, Chapter Six, the Sermon on the Mount. He came to the Lord's Prayer, the Our Father, in that chapter. When he had finished copying the Our Father, he had found it so beautiful that he wrote a little prayer in the margin next to it: "For thine is the kingdom, and the power, and the glory forever. Amen." This was a gloss, or marginal note, of type two.

Then when the next copyist came along and saw the gloss, he mistook it for a marginal note of type one—something left out by the previous copyist, and hence something he thought should be put back in.

So he copied it from the margin right into the words of the Our Father in the Gospel of Matthew itself. And the next copyist kept it there. And the next, and the next . . ., and before it was all over, there were more manuscripts in Christendom with this gloss mistakenly included in the text than manuscripts without it!

Scripture scholars of later times, though, whose job it was to reconstruct the correct words of the Bible by comparing whole "families" of manuscripts, among the dozens of other things they do to make sure our bibles are right, discovered the error, and that phrase is no longer in the Bible. Now it is our own little prayer that we add to the Lord's prayer, just as that unknown copyist of long ago did, his heart smitten with the beauty of the prayer Jesus himself had composed.

This is just one more example of the interesting work done by Scripture scholars, the people who, among other things, study ancient manuscripts of the Bible. There are many more examples that we could give. But now it is time to look at some of the facts about particular parts of the Bible, as they were transmitted down through the centuries "written by hand." And we shall begin with the way the Hebrew Bible—most of the Old Testament—was copied from manuscript to manuscript.

Manuscript History of the Hebrew Bible

The books of the Bible that had been originally written in Hebrew—most of the Old Testament, as we have seen—were copied and recopied, down through the generations, as more copies were needed or as the old ones began to crumble to dust. As we know, all the copying was done by hand, letter by letter, and changes crept in all along the way, so that Scripture scholars today have to sort out what the "correct" original reading was, by comparing manuscripts that still exist and can be read. And, of course, we also know that all this is true of any of the books of the Bible, not just of the books that were originally written in Hebrew. But there are certain interesting things about the Hebrew books of the Bible that are not true of most of the other books of the Bible.

One particularly interesting fact is that, no matter how far back into history scholars can trace, most of the books of the Bible tend to exist in different versions. It would be as if you had half-a-dozen editions of a modern book, each rather different from the others.

How is this to be explained? The answer is a mystery. This is something Scripture scholars will have to work on and tell us the answer. But here is one possibility: The books of the Hebrew Bible may have had a much longer, richer, more varied oral tradition than the other books of the Bible. In other words, these books may have been recited in the clan from grandfathers to children for so many generations and by so many different groups of people that by the time they came to be written down for the first time, they were written down in different wordings.

Then something even more unusual happened. Beginning a little over a thousand years ago, suddenly just the opposite began to occur. From the late A.D. 800s onward, copyists were so careful and transmitted all the books of the Hebrew Bible so accurately that not a single important change is to be found from one scroll to another all the way to the invention of printing! This time we know what the reason was: A group of Jews called the Masoretes, or "traditionalists," who lived in the A.D. 600s to 800s in Palestine, had such respect and love for the word of God as shown to them in the Bible that they not only copied each scroll with almost superhuman care, but passed down their spirit of love and care to all the Jewish copyists to come after them. And this same love for and attention to the word of God can still be observed in the synagogues of our present day.

Another interesting fact that is special to the Hebrew Bible is that ancient Hebrew was written entirely with consonants. There were no vowels in the Hebrew alphabet. Anyone who could read knew where the vowels went. Wouldn't you, in English? Suppose our bibles began this way: *n th bgnnng Gd crtd hvn nd rth.* If you were used to reading sentences without vowels, and had read them all your life, and had never even seen a vowel because there was no way to write one, you would have little trouble pronouncing this sentence correctly as: "In the beginning God created heaven and earth."

People in ancient times, then, had no trouble reading the Hebrew Bible if they could read Hebrew at all. Of course, most people could not read or write anyway, and only *heard* the Old Testament, in the Temple, or at another gathering, and eventually in the gathering that came to be called "synagogue" (from the Greek *syn-,* "together," and *-agog-,* "to lead"—"to lead together," or "gather").

People today who, like ourselves, live in a land where nearly everyone can read and write are often surprised to learn that "general literacy"—nearly everyone knowing how to read and write—is a product of modern times and is limited to certain modern countries. In some countries today very few people can read or write. This was the case in all countries in ancient times. Knowing how to read and write, or "literacy," in those days, was only about as common as someone having an advanced college degree today.

There were two reasons for this. First, the common people in ancient times, no matter in what civilization, worked fourteen to eighteen hours a day, from before they were twelve years old. And they didn't "retire" until they became sick or feeble or died. They simply were not allowed time to learn to read or write.

Second, there were very few "books" in ancient times. Books had to be copied by hand—from scroll to scroll—and this made them extremely precious and expensive, so that only the very rich had them. Of course, a large group of people might get together and all own a book. This explains why a synagogue (community of Jews) or church (community of Christians) would have a bible, or most of a bible—a set of scrolls—while individuals had none. In other words, individuals were too poor and too illiterate to read the Bible. But groups could afford one copy and could find some one person to read aloud to the others when all were gathered in worship.

To return, then, to our story of the Hebrew Bible in manuscript: The Jews of very ancient times had no problem with a bible which had no vowels, because a scholar, who knew how to read, such as a rabbi (which means "teacher") would read it to them.

But the day eventually came when even literate

Jews no longer knew their Hebrew very well. Even in the time of Jesus, Hebrew was not the language that Jewish people spoke at home or on the street. They still *heard* Hebrew, of course, in synagogue, when they listened to the Bible being read. But in their everyday lives they spoke Aramaic, a language that had come from Hebrew, somewhat as modern English comes from Old English and Old French. English-speaking people today are unable to understand Old English or Old French without special training.

Now, if even in the first century, people had begun to forget their Hebrew, we are not surprised to learn that people in later times forgot it even more. And so the day came when Hebrew had to be learned by Jews in school. Now a Hebrew bible written only in consonants would no longer do.

And so it came about that during the period from A.D. 600 to 800, the Masoretes—the traditionalist Jewish Scripture scholars living in Palestine—began to copy their scrolls with consonants *and* vowels. This made reading easier for people whose Hebrew was good enough to understand the words when they were actually pronounced but who did not know enough Hebrew to know exactly how they were to be pronounced. Now Jews had scrolls of the Bible from which they could actually teach Hebrew, and this they did.

But the Masoretes inserted their vowels in a way that will strike us as very curious. Remember, there are no vowels in the Hebrew alphabet. This is why there had been no vowels in the Hebrew Bible, of course. And the Masoretes were unwilling to invent letters to represent vowels—"Masorete" means "traditionalist," remember, and Masoretes wanted to keep God's Word, all God's words, every single one, just the way they were. And yet they wanted to find *some* way of showing vowels in words. So instead of using letters for vowels, the Masoretes showed the vowels as little dots and lines above and below the consonants! The Word of God was too sacred to be tampered with, they thought. We need vowels, they said, but we don't want to change the holy word. So we'll write the vowels as little, unobtrusive signs, above and below the big, beautiful consonants that represent the word of God. This is why, even today, sometimes you will see Hebrew words with dots and lines above or below the letters, and sometimes you will not.

Another advantage to this way of writing vowels, of course, was that it could be used with older scrolls, scrolls which had been written without vowels, and without any thought of vowels ever being written. There was no room between the letters. But there was room above and beneath.

We are not surprised to know that the scholars who did this, the Masoretes, were the same ones as those who so suddenly in the A.D. 800s began the nearly perfect copying of the Bible that yielded almost no mistakes over the next six hundred years! Yes, the Masoretes must have loved the Word of God intensely. And many Jews today still love not just God's message, but the words themselves that the message comes in. "The letter of the law" means the letters of the words in the Law, the Torah. We have the expression even in English.

The Qumran Scrolls

There are dozens of things we could say about Hebrew Bible manuscripts, some of them very interesting. But we do not have space for many more examples. Perhaps some of our readers will do further Scripture study some day by taking college courses in Scripture or joining Bible study clubs. Then there will be many, many interesting, fascinating things to learn about the Bible.

But there is one thing about Hebrew Bible manuscripts that we must certainly not leave out. It is surely the most exciting thing about Hebrew manuscripts to have happened in our times. It is the discovery of the Qumran scrolls.

One day in the late 1940s, some shepherds found some strange writing in a cave in a cliff above the Dead Sea in Palestine. The cave was full of these old papers, the shepherds said. And sure enough, when Scripture scholars (many of whom are archeologists, persons who dig up the remnants of ancient civilizations) checked in the cave and in nearby caves, they came upon the most marvelous cache of manuscripts that anyone has found for a thousand years.

This happened just a few decades ago. Scholars have still not pieced together, or even catalogued, all the manuscripts and pieces of manuscripts in this fantastic "find." There must have been fragments of nearly 300 different manuscripts in Qumran! There is one manuscript of the whole Book of Isaiah. Some of these manuscripts date from 300 years before Jesus—before the Old Testament was all written! Scholars are of course most interested in exactly what these manuscripts say. None of the little changes that can creep into manuscripts in the course of 2,000 years can possibly have crept into *these* old manuscripts! They were lost for these 2,000 years! Perhaps the wording in some of the manuscripts will some day give us the words of the original Old

Testament even more accurately than Scripture scholars and copyists have passed them down to us so far. But this is the exciting work of today's Scripture scholars, and most of us will just have to wait and see. (And who knows? Are there still other undiscovered Bible manuscripts somewhere in some forgotten hiding place, waiting to be discovered?)

Printed Hebrew Bibles

As soon as the printing press had been invented in the A.D. 1400s, parts of the Old Testament began to be printed in Hebrew for use in synagogues and by Jewish Scripture scholars. At first, whenever any part of the Bible was printed on a press in Hebrew, an explanation, or "commentary," was printed on the same pages—somewhat like the "fine print" on the pages of our English bibles, which explain things about this particular page of the Bible that otherwise only Scripture scholars would know.

The first Hebrew Bible the Christians printed was a "polyglot" Bible—from the Greek *poly-*, "many," and *-glott-*, "language." This huge Bible, in six volumes, contained the Old Testament not only in Hebrew but in Latin, Greek, and Aramaic (the language of Jesus) as well. The reason Latin was included was mostly to help Christian scholars sharpen up their Hebrew. Christians west of the Adriatic Sea were good at Latin, for Latin had become the language of the Western Roman Empire in the early Christian centuries; and the Roman Empire itself had become Christian in the A.D. 300s and 400s. But Christians were not so good at Hebrew. Ever since this fantastic six-volume polyglot Bible appeared, however, in the early A.D.

1500s, Christian Scripture scholars have been very good at Hebrew, because this Bible not only made it easy for them to understand the Hebrew—all they had to do was look at the Latin next to it—but it also gave them the taste for reading the Old Testament in its original language. It showed them the pleasure of reading the Old Testament in the very words people had first heard it, two thousand years before.

Scripture scholars still publish polyglot bibles today, and for the same two reasons. It helps people to learn Hebrew and Greek: All readers have to do is look at the English next to them, provided they have already begun to study Hebrew or Greek, and they can see what each word must mean. And it gives people the pleasure of reading the Bible in its original language. If you live near a college library or big city library, you may be able to find a polyglot Bible right there on the shelves.

The Septuagint

An old legend tells how Ptolemy II, mighty king of Egypt in the 200s B.C., demanded to know what the Jewish Scriptures said, for many Jews were subjects of his, and he wanted to know enough about them to guarantee their loyalty. So he wished to know what they believed.

So Ptolemy called for a translation of the Hebrew Bible into his own language, Greek. But he was afraid of being fooled. He was afraid the translators might leave something out or put something extra in, or change something, just to please him, and hide what they really believed. Ptolemy wanted to know exactly what the Old Testament said, however, word for word. Then he had an idea. He would employ a number of translators and have them all translate the same books—and their translations had better come out pretty much the same! Of course, he could not expect them to come out *exactly* the same, because no two translators ever translate a long passage exactly the same. A translator normally has to make many choices among various possible words to get just the right shade of meaning. A translation is a personal affair, to a certain extent, because individuals will make different choices of just what word to use. For example, one translator might translate a foreign word as "country," while another might choose "land" instead.

Well, Ptolemy sent to Jerusalem for seventy translators, we are told, and when they came he locked each of them up in solitary confinement! Now they could not connive—they could not agree on how to fool the king by falsifying any of the translation. And each was kept locked up until he had translated the whole Hebrew Torah, the first five books of the Bible. When they were all finished, he released them and took the seventy torahs, and—lo and behold—the translations not only generally agreed, but by some miracle were word-for-word the same!

Today we look upon this story as a legend. But it gives us an insight into the tremendous respect Jews had for the word of God to begin with—and then for the Greek translation they had composed this legend about. The Word of God was originally in Hebrew, of course—but God must have had a hand in this Greek translation of the Seventy, as well, Jews thought. (The Latin word for "seventy" is *septuagint-*.)

Eventually, all the books of the Hebrew Bible were translated into Greek, and the whole translation came to be called the Septuagint, even though only the Torah had originally been translated.

Six-Ply Bible of the Man of Steel

Greek continued to be the main language of the Roman Empire for several centuries, especially in the eastern half—east of the Adriatic sea. Christians, who were multiplying rapidly in that empire, needed to read the Old Testament in Greek, then. Of course, they had always read the *New* Testament in Greek: It had been written in Greek in the first place.

So as Christians multiplied, Greek translations of the Old Testament multiplied, and the situation became confusing. By the A.D. 200s, people had begun to wonder which Greek translation was "right." No two translators ever use exactly the same words, of course. And besides, some translated from some Hebrew manuscripts and some from others, and the manuscripts they translated from were surely all a little different from one another. So which one was closest to the original Hebrew?

Then the great Origen came along. Origen is easily the greatest Scripture scholar and biblical theologian of the first Christian centuries. In fact, he is doubtless the greatest theologian (philosopher of the faith) of those centuries.

Origen determined to study the Bible in a way that strikes us as very modern and scholarly for those ancient days. He composed a polyglot Old Testament—1300 years before the first great *printed* polyglot Old Testament, which we have already mentioned. First he copied by hand, with the help of his students, the Hebrew Bible in a narrow column on a scroll, and another scroll, and another and another, until the whole Hebrew Old Testament had been copied down in Hebrew. Then he made a second column alongside the first, putting down all the same words as in the first column—but in Greek letters! Now anyone could look at any Hebrew word and pronounce it without even knowing Hebrew—just by looking at the same word in Greek letters and pronouncing *that*! Now he had two columns on each of his scrolls.

Then he put four more columns in—four different Greek translations of the first column (one was the Septuagint). So then he had columns three, four, five, and six, and anyone who looked at a scroll could not only pronounce the Hebrew but could see what it meant in Greek. And in the same glance, anyone could see all the differences among the four Greek translations!

Now Origen had a great scholarly work lying before him. This was the famous *hexapla,* or "six-layer" Bible, and people came from all over the world to consult it. Anyone who came to Origen's library could look up any part of the Old Testament, look at the Hebrew in one column, see how it was pronounced in the second column, and then take his or her pick of four Greek translations—or five or six or seven, since Origen sometimes added other translations when the differences among them were particularly interesting. As we have seen, there were felt to be almost too many Greek translations of the Hebrew Bible going around, each a little different from the others.

Origen was a most remarkable person. He was head of the great School of Religious Instruction in Alexandria, in Egypt, at the mouth of the Nile.

Alexandria in those days was the second-greatest city in the world; only Rome was greater. In fact, there was more trade and perhaps more intellectual life going on in Alexandria than in Rome. Origen had taken over the School of Religious Instruction when its founder, his teacher, had been forced to flee the city because of Roman persecutions of religion teachers. (Not the pupils, just the teachers. The Romans thought this would be the easy way to cut Christianity off so that it would die out. It didn't work.) Origen, however, refused to leave town. He wanted to be a martyr (the Greek word for "witness," meaning "witness for Christ"). He wanted to suffer and die for Christ. In fact, whenever other teachers were on trial or were about to be executed, Origen was right there at their side, encouraging them to die bravely for Jesus. He hoped that this behavior would provoke the Romans into taking *him* and executing him for Jesus. In fact, the story is told of the night Origen bid his mother farewell forever; he was going to join the glorious ranks of the martyrs on the following day. But when he got up in the morning he found that his mother had hidden all his clothes, and he certainly couldn't go to his martyrdom with no clothes on! And so there was nothing to do but go on teaching Christ, instead of dying for him.

One of the most interesting things about Origen is that he was a teenager during this persecution, when he took over the School. Surely, then, he was one of the most remarkable teenagers who ever lived. He did not get his wish for martyrdom, not yet. He had many years to live first, and he would have to witness to Jesus by scholarship first. The persecution was over.

Origen used his remaining years—half a century of them!—to study the Bible with the same enthusiasm, energy, creative imagination, and plain hard work as he had shown when he had first taken over the School. They called him *Calch-Enteros*— "Bowels of Brass." (My, how people came right out and said things in those days! Let's just say "Man of Steel.") He wrote dozens of books. Unfortunately, however, nearly one hundred percent of what he wrote is lost today. Even his six-ply Bible is lost— crumbled to dust and never recopied again. For it so happened that three hundred years after Origen's death, in the middle of the A.D. 200s, the Church condemned some followers of his for what it considered to be a false religious teaching—a "heresy." (Heresy comes from the Greek word *hairēsis,* meaning "choosing," for some people were accused of "picking and choosing" the things they believed about God and Christ instead of listening to the Church.) So three hundred years after they were written, Origen's books were destroyed or allowed to crumble to dust, even though they contained no heresy themselves, just to emphasize the condemnation of his followers. His magnificent Bible escaped at first, but only for about a hundred years, and today only fragments remain.

How did Origen manage to do so much writing? He couldn't have had a word processor, or even a typewriter. Did he have a secretary?

Yes, he had a secretary, and then some. A wealthy friend of the School of Religious Instruction, we are told, hired seven stenographers to work for Origen and take his dictation. Then, as each stenographer filled a page with the shorthand of those days, he would go off and redictate Origen's words to a long-hand copyist, while Origen went on with the next stenographer . . . and so on, until he had dictated something to all seven. Then he would start over with stenographer number one.

Meanwhile, Origen's rich friend had also hired enough young ladies to copy out the longhand writing in "calligraphy" (from the Greek *kall-*, "beautiful," and *-graph-*, "writing")—that is, in nice, finished form, with each letter of the alphabet drawn perfectly by hand. And lo and behold, the Man of Steel and his triple team of stenographers, longhand copyists, and calligraphers produced a manuscript. Then they made another. And another, and another, and another.

As an old man of seventy, Origen the Man of Steel had his teenage prayer answered, and he died a martyr for the faith of Christ—as gladly as he had lived for Christ, we are told. And yet he had never seen Jesus in the flesh. He had read about him in the Bible.

Latin Translations of the Old Testament

Latin, the language of the ancient Romans, eventually became the universal language of the Roman Empire. After the fall of the Empire, it was still the official language of the Christian Church, and this it remained until the coming of the Protestant Reformers in the A.D. 1500s. Latin is still the official language of the Roman Catholic Church, although it has almost entirely disappeared from church services in favor of the "vernacular," the ordinary spoken language of the people in the congregation.

But it took a long time for Latin to become the official language of the Empire and the Church. Most of the people who lived in the Empire were nonRomans, and the language they spoke in order to be understood by people of other nationalities in the Empire was usually Greek, the language of the people who had ruled the eastern Mediterranean before the Romans came.

Still, the Romans *had* come and conquered the "world"—the Mediterranean world. (This was the only world our Western civilization knew then, or the only one it considered of any importance.) And Latin became the universal language in the western half of that "world" (leaving Greek in the eastern half). By the A.D. 200s, most people in the western half of the Roman Empire, or "Mediterranean world," knew some Latin, and some knew *only* Latin. So there arose a great demand for the Bible in Latin by the Christians and Jews among these people. And there were always more and more Christians among them.

The earliest Latin Old Testament—apparently translated from a Greek translation—seems to have been done by Jews in northern Africa in the late A.D. 100s. A thousand miles from Palestine, these Jews spoke neither Aramaic nor Greek, but Latin. So they needed the Bible in Latin.

But the most famous Latin translation was Saint Jerome's "Vulgate" Bible, or Common Translation—meaning translation "for everybody." This fiery-tempered hermit was the best Scripture scholar in the world, and Pope Damasus asked him to do a revision of the whole Latin Bible. So around the year 400, when Jerome was not squabbling with the pope about something, he could usually be found translating the Bible for him.

The Vulgate is a beautiful piece of writing. From the point of view of language, Saint Jerome's translation of the New Testament is actually more beautiful than most of the Greek he translated it from.

Saint Jerome's Vulgate Bible, his Latin translation of the Bible, ran into trouble at first. Just as happens today when a new translation of the Bible comes out, Saint Jerome's Bible just "didn't sound right" to some people. It "changed things," they said. After all, what people had been used to hearing was the Latin of some other translator. This new Latin sounded "funny"—as with our translations today, when instead of "He maketh me to lie down in green pastures," our parents and grandparents suddenly find themselves hearing, "In verdant pastures he gives me repose." And they say, *"That's* the *Bible*?"

Sure that's the Bible. Word for word. It's just a different translation, that's all. It means exactly the same thing. Both versions are from the first verse of the Twenty-Third Psalm, "The Lord is my shepherd." But people who are used to the old way often prefer the old way. Subconsciously, it reminds them of their childhood—the "good old days," when things were the way "they used to be." And just as our new English translations sometimes run into trouble this way, even when they are better, so Saint Jerome's Latin Vulgate ran into trouble, even though it was better.

In any case, this translation, in one form or another, became the official Bible of the Western Christian Church for nearly a thousand years and of the Catholic Church for *more* than a thousand years, right up to the middle of our own twentieth century!

English Translations of the Bible

England became Christian in the A.D. 200s, but there were no translations of any great part of the Bible in English until at least the year 1000. Church services, including the Eucharist, were in Latin, and so was the Bible that was read there. The only things people knew about the Bible was what they heard from their priests in sermons. This seems strange to us today. Apparently, people sincerely thought that they did not need to know what the actual words of the Bible *said,* as long as they had an educated, honest person, their priest, around to tell them what it *meant.* Of course, most people nowadays, too, would agree that the meaning of the Bible is more important than the mere words on the page. In fact, this is an important principle of biblical theology. But very few people today who care what the Bible is *about* would be willing to do without exactly what it *says.* There is no way for us today, in most of our English-speaking countries, to grasp the importance of "literacy"—knowing how to read and write. We are so used to being "literate" that we scarcely notice that we are! But more than ninety-nine percent of the people in days gone by were illiterate. And so there was no English Bible for nearly a thousand years after England had become Christian.

The first bible that was anything like a real English translation seems to have been made up of a number of "interlinear" translations of parts of the Bible, beginning in the A.D. 800s. "Interlinear" means "between the lines." A Latin manuscript would be copied in such a way as to leave enough space between the lines to put in the English words for the Latin words just above or below. Or else an old manuscript would be used, and the English words would be squeezed in small under the big Latin words that were already there. The purpose of the interlinear translations was actually more to teach Latin and to learn the Bible in Latin than to read the Bible in English.

So the first good English Bible did not come along until John Wycliffe and his team of scholars made one in the late A.D. 1300s. Wycliffe's translation was not generally used in church, though, because Wycliffe criticized church teachings, church beliefs—and that made his bible suspect in official eyes. So the Church not only forbade people to use Wycliffe's translation but also forbade anyone to make any more translations. It seemed safer to stay with the approved Latin. Still, Wycliffe's bible became very popular, because, once people had tasted the thrill of reading the Bible in their very own language, they wanted more and more of the experience.

In the A.D. 1500s, William Tyndale translated the New Testament into English directly from the Greek, instead of translating a Latin translation. He also translated a great deal of the Old Testament from a Latin translation of the Hebrew. He too got into trouble with the authorities, but his way of putting the words of the Bible into beautiful English remained a model for English translations of the Bible to imitate right up to our own times.

Other English translations followed. The printing press had been invented by then, and books no longer needed to be kept chained to library tables or millionaires' reading stands. People could have books of their own, and literacy grew by leaps and bounds.

King Henry VIII, who separated the Church of England from the Roman Catholic Church in the 1500s, ordered a copy of the Bible in English to be placed in every church in the land.

By the A.D. 1500s the Protestant Reformers were working and changing things all over "continental Europe" (Europe minus the British Isles). And one of the things the Protestants insisted on was having the Bible in the "vernacular"—the ordinary language of the people: German for the Germans, French for the French, and so on. Martin Luther was a great pioneer in this area, as in so many others.

By the late 1500s the vernacular movement could no longer be stopped. People were still often willing to hear the Bible in Latin in church, if they were Roman Catholics, especially if it was explained to them in the sermon or "homily" (a sermon that explains part of a Gospel that has just been read). But for use outside the Eucharist, even Catholics wanted to have the Bible in English. So Catholics made a translation called the Douay-Rheims version, from the two cities in which it was made (outside England—Catholicism was illegal in England). And this version remained the official English translation for Catholics until the middle of our twentieth century.

But the most loved English bible of all is the King James Version. It is not only very beautiful in its language, but its writers were the very best scholars available at the time, and they did a remarkable job of saying in English what the Hebrew or Greek of the original Bible actually says. King James I of England hired some fifty Scripture scholars for the task, and when the great bible was finished in the early 1600s, he made it the official bible of the Church of England. It was to be the great English bible for more than 400 years.

The great King James version came out in edition after edition, as more and more thousands of churches, libraries, and homes called for copies of this beautiful book. It was revised—that is, corrected and improved—several times too, and so we have the Revised Version, the American Standard Version, and the Revised Standard Version, all of which came out around A.D. 1900.

The New English Bible, the bible most used in English speaking lands today, is a completely new translation and not a simple revision of the King James version, as earlier English bibles had been. It puts the Bible in twentieth-century English, instead of Elizabethan English, the language of the King James Bible.

Catholics continued to publish their own translations with the New American Bible and the Jerusalem Bible (which was a translation of a great new French translation) in the middle A.D. 1900s, just a generation or so ago.

The English have sometimes had amusing nicknames for their translations of the Bible. One of the earliest translations is called the "Breeches Bible" (pronounced "britches"), because this is the word used to translate the first clothes Adam and Eve wore when they noticed they were naked! Then there is a "Vinegar Bible," so called because in one of Jesus' parables about a vineyard, "vineyard" in a title was misprinted as "vinegar." There is even a "Wicked Bible," so called because the printer absent-mindedly (we hope) left the word "not" out of the commandment, "Thou shalt not commit adultery." (He was fined heavily for the oversight.)

But British humor cannot conceal the great love of English-speaking people for their Bible. Their work in translating the world's best-seller, handing it on to us today down through the centuries in a language we can all read, and often a beautiful language as well, stands as one of the most remarkable monuments in the history of literature.

And Translations and Translations . . .

Naturally, we cannot take time to tell about all the translations in all the hundreds of languages in which the world's best-seller exists today. In fact, we have mentioned only a small proportion of the translations that were done in Greek, or Latin, or English. If we had more space, we could tell about the Japanese bible of the early A.D. 1600s, which seems to have been made by Jesuit priests who were seeking to convert Japan to Christianity. And we could go on and on. But we must stop now, and remind our reader that this chapter—like all the others—is just a foretaste of the wealth of knowledge about the Bible that may await him or her in the years to come.

5
Word of God, Word of Human Beings

A hundred generations of Jews and Christians have considered the Bible to be the inspired word of God. And Jews and Christians believe that their God knows all things and never lies. Therefore, Jews and Christians traditionally believe that the Bible must be true, every word.

Here, however, a problem seems to arise today, as it has arisen at other moments in Jewish and Christian history. Is every word of the Bible *literally* true? Or are the words of the Bible just "a way of saying things," so that what the Bible really means is not exactly what it says? And are there mistakes in the Bible?

As the great Saint Augustine, probably the most important thinker of the ancient Christian Church, pointed out: The Bible could not be *literally* true, every word, since sometimes it states things that everyone knows to be impossible. For example, Augustine reminds us, in the very first chapter of the Bible, Chapter One of the Book of Genesis, we read that God made day and night before he made sun or moon or stars! Understood literally, this would be nonsense, Augustine said. God's word must mean something else than what it literally seems to mean. At least that is what Augustine thought, and that is what many people today think.

There are other problems, too. There are not only questions of logic or fact; there are questions of morality. For instance, in the Books of Joshua and

Judges, the sixth and seventh books of the Bible, coming right after the Torah, we read that God commanded the armies of his people, when they conquered a city in war, to leave no survivors—to kill every man, woman, and child in the conquered town. This sounds much more like what human beings would do on their own than what God would want them to do.

Besides problems of fact and problems of morality, there are lesser problems, such as chronology, or order of time. For instance, one Gospel may say that Jesus did two things or went to two places in one order, and another Gospel may say that he did the two things or went to the two places in just the opposite order.

Also there are problems of precise quotation. For instance, one Gospel, or one book of the Old Testament, may report Jesus or Moses as saying something in certain words—and another Gospel or another book of the Old Testament may report him as using slightly different words. And again, all the evidence will seem to indicate that it is the same statement being reported.

And the "problems" abound. Evolutionists say the Bible contradicts evolution, so the Bible must be wrong. Fundamentalists agree that the Bible contradicts evolution, and say that evolution must be wrong.

There are other problems, too, of error, or apparent error, in the Bible. But they all come down to this: Let's grant that the Bible is certainly exciting, inspiring, and full of truth. *But if the Bible contains errors, how can it be the word of God?*

People of faith have struggled with this question

over the centuries. And they have given several answers. We shall give one of their answers here, and it will take the rest of this chapter. This answer is full of deep faith in the Bible as the word of God and yet at the same time respectful of modern scholarship and science. That is, it is a product of both *faith* and *reason*. Those who give this explanation believe that it is one and the same God who gives them their faith and their reason. The one God teaches them the truths they need for their salvation and gives them the possibility of creating human science. Faith and reason cannot be in contradiction, then, these people say. The Bible and science cannot contradict each other.

The answer to the question of how the Bible can seem to contain errors or make statements that are not literally true can be given in terms of (1) "literary genre" and (2) "inspiration."

Literary Genre

The people who give us this explanation of the seeming errors in the Bible believe that their God is almighty, that he can do anything he wishes to do. And certainly he can do anything that his creatures, human beings, can do.

Now if Leo Tolstoy or Ernest Hemingway, without being almighty, can write a short story or a novel, then certainly God can write a short story or a novel if he wishes. If a mere human being can write *War and Peace* or *For Whom the Bell Tolls,* which are books of fiction, but which reveal a great deal of truth about human life, then certainly God can write the book of Jonah—a book of fiction too, but divine fiction— which reveals a great deal about God's salvation.

A statement can be true, our explanation continues, without being materially true, without being mechanically true. In fact, if the statement is to be chock-full of truth, it might actually be better if it is *not* literally, mechanically, "factually" true. For the Bible is literature.

Let us take an example of this from purely human literature. Instead of writing his great novel, *War and Peace,* Leo Tolstoy could have simply told the history of some family he knew. He could have written a simple account of events he had remembered, or heard about, from his own life or from times past. But then he would never have created Natasha, the heroine of *War and Peace*. What gripping experiences Natasha lives! All around her, and in her heart as well, she lives a life of high adventure and so matures into a young woman. In other words, Tolstoy could of course have written about some "real" girl instead, but then he would not have created the girl who is somehow every girl who ever lived, and somehow every person who ever lived. Of course Tolstoy could have just told us the interesting adventure of, say, Vera Popova down the street, a girl who actually, physically, lived. Then his book would have been "true" because Vera is a real, historical girl. But Vera is not *you*! Natasha *is* you, the reader. This was Tolstoy's genius—to be able to make up a fictional character who was "truer than true"—a character who may not have lived physically but who lives inside all of us, just waiting to be let out and be talked about. By creating the lovely literary character of Natasha, Tolstoy created a personage who was, is, and always will *be* the millions of readers who read about her as they share her joys and sufferings. Her joys and sufferings are just like yours! And how beautifully she overcomes them! So can you! Not true? Of course Natasha is true. She never once existed. Never once—only millions of times.

No one wishes Tolstoy had written a "true" story. Anybody can do that. People are glad he wrote a novel instead—because, lo and behold, there is more truth about life and about you in his novel than in any "true" story most people have ever read.

Now, if Tolstoy can do this, then certainly God can. Of course the story of Jonah and the great fish *could have* been literally true—historically true, factually true. There *is* a fish big enough to swallow a man, and it lives in the Mediterranean, where Jonah's fish swam. But this is not the point, say the people whose explanation we are examining. All the evidence we have, say Scripture scholars, points to the Book of Jonah as being not literal history but a made-up story. So much the better, say the people whose explanation we are examining. (They are called "biblical theologians," or scholars who try to understand the Bible's actual meaning for faith and life by using human reason to help their divine faith.) So much the better! So God has made up a story! What a wonderful story it must be, then! It must be beautiful, and it must really get its message across. That is, it must be chock-full of truth—at least as much truth as in *War and Peace*!

In the story of Jonah, in the Old Testament, God commands Jonah to go and preach to the people of the city of Nineveh, who are not Jews, and who therefore do not seem to belong to God's chosen people. So Jonah says no, he will not go and preach to them. But God says, "You *shall* go, Jonah." And

103

God has the great fish swallow him whole and carry him to the shores of Nineveh. There the great fish spews Jonah out onto the sand as if he were being born again—born from some dark, watery womb of ignorance. For he learns in spite of himself that God is God for these people too. God must love these people too. So Jonah goes and preaches to the people of Nineveh. God loves *all* people and all peoples.

And we who read the story learn that God is the God of *all* peoples, and that if one is a special Chosen People, it must be because they have a special job—to carry God's word to all other peoples!

Not a true story? Of course it is a true story, say our biblical theologians. It is not *historically* true, it is not *literally* true—it did not simply happen at one time and in one place. But it is *universally* true; that is, it is happening in all times and all places! It is true for Jews, for Catholics, and Protestants, and Muslims, and members of the traditional religions of Africa, and . . . well, it is true for everyone that if God chooses a special people, it is because he wants them to carry his message to others and not just keep it for themselves, as old Jonah had wanted to. The Book of Jonah not a true story? Of course it is a true story. It was true when it was written, and it is true today. It is true right within my heart right now, for I am some-one who is really not entirely willing to carry God's love to peoples who seem strange to me, and for whom I feel a dislike—as Jonah did for the Nine-vites. I am Jonah, in a way, then; and as I read the Book of Jonah, I can experience a spiritual rebirth in my heart as Jonah is reborn from the belly of the great fish; and I can go out and do something for the "ugly stranger" whom God loves so much.

This is the explanation these particular biblical theologians give us of how the Bible can contain fiction. And they give us their explanation in such a way that we can tell they are actually *glad* that the Book of Jonah is not a mere "true story"—they are glad that it is a piece of the truth itself, something that is true for everybody. It is a good thing that God can write fiction, these biblical theologians say. It is no coincidence that it is a wonderful story. Look who wrote it!

You see, biblical theologians today say that there are several different "literary genres" in the Bible. *Genre* in French means "kind," or "type." "Literary genre" means "kind or type of writing." (*Genre* is usually pronounced jän-rĕ in English.) As applied to the Bible, the concept of literary genre means that there are different types of writing in the Bible, some of which were never intended to be taken literally. "I am a flower of Sharon, a lily of the valley," says the beloved in the Song of Songs. Surely she is not *literally* a flower. This is metaphor; this is poetry. Can God not write poetry? Creatures can; why not their Creator? And just as there is poetry in the Bible, so are there other literary genres not meant to be taken literally or that are not mechanically true in the way a book of chemistry or history might be true.

And yes, then, there is fiction in the Bible— excellent fiction, full of salvation truths, God's own creative, picturesque message to human beings, God's own short stories and novels. There is poetry, as we have just seen. There is saga—history, yes, but history embellished with heroic imagination and marvelous happenings, as in the Books of Joshua and Judges.

There is even myth in the Bible—as in the first chapter of the Book of Genesis, when God made all the stars in one day and flung them out into his new universe for his creatures' admiration and wonder; or when he made his human creature out of mud with his own hands. As the old play, *Green Pastures,* puts it, God knelt down there in the mud and cradled his new creature in his arms "like an old mammy" cradling her lovely baby, so much did he love him and her, the human being he had thought up. And many of these myths were even partly borrowed from the writings of Israel's pagan neighbors—God "quoting from another author," you might say. Why not? If God's myth is fiction full of truth—glorious myth about our glorious God and about God's special plan for the happiness of each and all of us—then, why not? biblical theologians ask. Human beings write myths. Perhaps God wrote the best one of all, the one with the most truth about life and death, and everlasting life.

Finally—lest we forget!—another literary genre in the Bible is: history. Just plain history, where what is told *is* plain, simple, literal fact, just "the way it was," with no fiction about it—like Mark's story of the crucifixion of Jesus.

Inspiration and Errors in the Bible

But an explanation of the literary genres in the Bible does not solve all our problems. It explains how God may perfectly well be the author of fiction—fiction packed with truth—but it does not explain how God may have been the author of an outright mistake.

For, our biblical theologians admit, there do seem to be mistakes in the Bible. The Acts of the Apostles makes mistakes about the geography of Palestine. The Gospel According to John says Jesus suffered and died a day later than the Synoptic Gospels do. And so on and on.

The problem is even more serious when the mistake is a moral mistake: when the Bible seems to command immorality, or reports that God commanded immorality—commanded someone to do something evil, something wrong. For instance, we have noticed in the Old Testament that God is said to have commanded his people to slaughter innocent foreigners. Or in the New Testament, Saint Paul, *the* Apostle, clearly considers women to be somehow inferior to men.

Our biblical theologians explain these difficulties with their theory of *biblical inspiration,* or "principal and instrumental authorship." God is only the principal author of the Bible, say our theologians. There were other authors too—the "instrumental authors" of the Bible (from the Latin *instrumentum,* "tool")— its human authors.

And our theologians explain their theory in this way: When *you* write something, you need a "tool," an instrument, do you not?—a pencil, a pen, a typewriter, or a word processor. Now, does the tool you use make a difference as to what comes out? Well, yes and no. It makes no difference to your *meaning,* but it certainly makes a difference in the *form* your meaning is in. If you use a smudgy pencil, your great thoughts may come out in smudgy writing. There is no way around that.

Well, say our biblical theologians, when God wrote the Bible he used tools too. Only God's tools were people. God had various human beings write his message down in all the various books of the Bible until he had everything necessary for our salvation in black and white. But the human beings he used were all different from one another. Some were historians, and God used them to write history. Some, like King David, were poets, and God used them to write poetry. Some were fine short-story writers or novelists, and God used them to write his wonderful fiction with all its truth. And finally . . . some were like pencils: they smudged. They made mistakes. They said God commanded the killing of innocent human beings when he didn't. They said women were inferior when they aren't. But if you clean up the smudges, biblical theologians say—if you sort out the human mistakes from the divine truth—then you have God's message.

Of course, there is a danger here. Again, let us take the example of your own writing with a tool. Suppose you write a brilliant essay for a school class, but you use a pencil and it smudges. It's really a great story—but what will your teacher do? (1) Your teacher may become disgusted and give up and give you a low grade; or (2) your teacher may not give up, and may try to go ahead and read your smudged writing anyway, but may misunderstand what you meant to say because it was too hard to read, and may therefore say you made mistakes and give you a bad grade anyway.

Of course, there is a third possibility: If the only thing you *had* was a pencil, your teacher (3) may not be disgusted at all, may work a little extra hard to try to see what you really mean in all that smudginess, and may see how wonderful it is, and give you a good grade—the one you deserved!

It is somewhat the same with the Bible, say the people who give the explanation we are examining. God didn't use a pencil or a pen or a typewriter or a word processor; he used people. He used smart people, dumb people, good writers, bad writers, apparently even good people and bad people!

In other words: No matter how wonderful a writer you are, if you use a dull pencil it may smudge. And even though God is all-wise and all-good, when he uses an "instrument" that is not very "sharp"—a human being who is not a very intelligent or very loving person—to write a book of his bible, God's wonderful message will come out smudged with mistakes: mistakes of fact, and even moral mistakes, because of the weakness of his instrument.

And then what happens? Well, (1) some people grow disgusted with the mistakes and make up their minds that it's not God's writing at all. They make no effort to see what God is really trying to say to us in the human words of a poor human being—what his message of salvation is "between the lines," as the saying goes. And they refuse to read or believe the Bible.

And (2) some people go ahead and read the Bible anyway, but they misunderstand the message because they get the wrong message. They get the human shell instead of the divine kernel. For example, someone reading the "instrumental author" who said that God commanded his people to kill their captives might conclude that it is all right for believers to kill helpless human beings in the name of God. It happens all the time! All you need to do is turn on the news.

But (3) there is another way to do it, our biblical

theologians tell us. Don't be turned off and don't give up. Read the Bible anyway. Try to sort out the mistakes the human authors wrote into the marvelous message of love and rescue that God is sending in these poor, weak human words.

There is plenty of help available—beginning with the "fine print" on the pages of our bibles. And then there are many interesting books *about* the Bible. And there are Bible classes. And everywhere there are people who are doing very much to help us sort out what God means in the Great Book he wrote, from what human beings may have done to smudge that meaning. It can be a very exciting search, and people have hours of enjoyment doing it.

After all, even the language in some books of the Bible is better than in others. "If you don't admit the Holy Spirit used poor Greek in Mark's Gospel and good Greek in Luke's, then you don't know Greek" is how one Scripture scholar put it. But that's not so bad. It's worse when we read a disgusting, sexist remark like "A woman's nagging is like a dripping gutter," from the book of Proverbs. How much more beautiful something like, "Set me like a seal on your arm, for love is strong as death." It may take some real biblical theology to get behind the foolishness of the human writer in the line about the gutter, in order to see what God really meant.

This is how biblical theologians tell us we have to go about understanding the Bible. And they guarantee us hours of profit and enjoyment. After all, they say, this Bible may be the word of human beings, but it is the word of God, too.

One mystery remains. If God is almighty—if he can do anything he wishes to—then *why did he choose to use human authors who were not always very intelligent or very moral as his tools in writing such an important thing as the Bible?* Ah, our biblical theologians tell us, this is the most amazing and exciting thing of all. He chose poor instruments as well as good instruments to show that his message of salvation is universal. His message is for all cultures, all degrees of intelligence, and even for both good people and bad. God wants to save all human beings who have ever lived, or ever will live, no matter who they are. And so he deliberately expresses his message of rescue in words produced in different cultures, by people of varying degrees of intelligence and goodness and badness. And he expects us to acquire the wisdom to know the difference. For he inspired them all to write exactly what each one wrote, each in each one's own way.

Epilogue

Lord, I Have Loved Your Law . . .

The Bible is the most loved book in the Western world. For some—for very many—it is the inspired word of God as well.

But what does it really do for people? How do people use it? What is it good for? If it is such a wonderful thing—especially if it is the word of God—it must have a purpose.

Of course, answering all these questions would take another book. The Bible is used for dozens and dozens of things. But we thought we should not close our study of "what the Bible is" without seeing *something* of what it is for, or what it is used for. We shall take each of the four great religious groups that use the Bible—Jews, Eastern Christians, Catholics, and Protestants—and examine just one thing that is typical of each group in its use of the Bible.

Lesson from Jews

For Jews, the Bible is God's pledge of loyalty to his Covenant with them, his sacred contract. And it is their pledge of loyalty to God. He is their God, they say, and they are his people.

As we have seen, the Torah, the Law—the first five Books of the Bible—holds an altogether special place in Jewish tradition. The Torah *is* the Covenant. And this is why a copy of the whole Torah, written by hand on a scroll as in olden days, is kept in every synagogue and is considered the holiest thing there.

112

It is housed in the "Ark" (the word means the "Vessel," or sacred container)—the name given to the portable little sacred house that the Jews carried with them in their wanderings in Bible times and that contained the stone tablets given them by God through Moses with the Ten Commandments on them. The glory of God dwelt in the Ark, the Bible says, just as the stone tablets did, for the words of the Lord and the Lord himself are very much the same in the Hebrew heart. The Ark was so sacred that no person dared touch it. And this tradition, this feeling of love and reverence for God's word almost as if for God himself, still surrounds the Torah today in synagogues all over the world, more than two thousand years after it was written.

Jews even have a special feast day, or holiday, once a year in honor of the Torah. The day is called Shimkath Torah, or the "Rejoicing in the Law." On this day each year, the Torah is taken from the Ark, and not just read from (as it is read from every Sabbath and feast day all year round, so that it is read in its entirety every year)—but danced with! Yes, on the holiday of the Torah, the sacred books are placed in the arms of one member of the synagogue after another, and all who hold the Lord's law to their heart dance and smile and show their gladness about their Covenant with God. For the Torah tells what Jewish religion is all about: God's liberation of his people from slavery in Egypt under the Pharaoh, the people's escape across the waters of the sea, to begin their journey to the promised land. And Jews believe God will always save his people at the last. Not even the Holocaust—the Nazi slaughter of six million Jews during World War II, along with millions of other victims—has destroyed Jews' faith in God's promise.

Lesson from Eastern Christians

As Jews show special reverence for the Torah in their synagogues, so Christians show special reverence for the Bible in their churches. This reverence stands out in a special way in Eastern Christians' behavior toward the Book of the Gospels—the most sacred thing lying on their altars, for it is a volume containing the Gospels According to Matthew, Mark, Luke, and John (and nothing else). It is the volume containing Jesus, then. For, just as God's word, for the Jews, is practically identical with God himself, as far as we human beings are concerned—so Jesus' word, for Eastern Christians, is practically identical with Jesus himself, who is called the Word of God.

Eastern Christians are the perhaps two hundred million Christians who live, or whose ancestors lived, east of the Adriatic Sea, from Yugoslavia and Greece to Russia and Finland, then down to Armenia and over to India and back to Egypt and Ethiopia, with practically every country in between. Most, but not all, are called "Orthodox Christians."

The Book of the Gospels is often very lavishly ornamented in the Christian East and is permanently kept on the altar, for it "is" Jesus, the Victim sacrificed for love in their Eucharist. During the Eucharist itself, the Book of the Gospels is carried in procession as if it were a king. The deacon holds the book high—against his forehead, perhaps, for he hopes its wisdom will enter into him and into all the people. And "Wisdom!" is the only word he sings.

Just as Passover—which commemorates the night

God led the Jews out of Egypt to freedom—is the Feast of Feasts for the Jews, so the Feast of Feasts for Christians is Easter, the day Jesus rose from the dead. Among Catholics and Protestants, the relatively new feast day called Christmas (dating only from the A.D. 300s) has stolen some of Easter's thunder, so to speak. Ask nearly any Catholic or Protestant—that is, nearly any Western Christian—what his or her greatest religious day is, and he or she might be tempted to answer, "Christmas." But this is not the traditional Christian answer, and Christians of the East make no mistake: The Day of Days is Easter, and the Night of Nights is the night before.

Eastern Christians traditionally celebrate Easter with a joy and gladness rarely equalled by Christians elsewhere. Singing "Christ is risen!" in a blazing sea of candles, the crowds push forward toward the altar as the priests, deacons, and other ministers come toward them bearing the sacred things of the church for the people to kiss. All smiles, the clergy cry, "Christ is risen!" And the people shout back "Truly risen!" And they too smile. Then they kiss the sacred objects of the church, such as the chalice used to hold the wine that for them is the saving blood of Jesus.

But the sacred object that is at the center of it all is the Book of the Gospels. For Eastern Christians, kissing the Book of the Gospels is like kissing their great friend himself, welcoming him back to new life from the tomb. And the singing is like the voice of angels. Russian church music, especially, may be the most beautiful and most prayerful church music in the world.

Then clergy and people kiss. Finally, all the people

kiss one another—three kisses, right on the lips; and nobody is embarrassed, because this is the Night of Nights, and the Rising Sun is Jesus himself, and we are all his! There's no room for shyness. And each person says "Christ is risen!" to the others, and the response is "Truly risen!" from everybody to everybody, on the Feast of Feasts in a world of burning lights.

In the Soviet Union, where dozens of millions of Eastern Christians—Russian Orthodox—live, but where so many churches have been closed or converted into museums, the people are too numerous to fit into the churches on the great feast of Easter. So they often have to crowd onto the steps outside. There, of course, they cannot see a thing. Ah, but they can hear. And when the sacred instant comes, after midnight, and all are holding candles lighted (even outside)—the cry "Christ is risen!" goes thundering through the crowd in the church and out the door and down the steps and into the street. Then the kiss of new life, too, rolls in a wave from the altar through the church and out the door and down the steps and into the street—the kiss that began with the Book of the Gospels, in which Jesus himself is the Word of God.

Lesson from Catholics

Most of our readers may be more familiar with Catholic and Protestant attitudes toward the Bible than they are with Jewish or Eastern Christian ones. But we can still pick out something special about the Catholics and something special about the Protestants with regard to the Bible.

Here again, as with Jews and Eastern Christians,

the problem is what to pick out, for there are so many things we could say. But for Catholics, we might say that they have a lesson for us in the way they do theology. Just as Protestants have taught Catholics much about Scripture scholarship, so Catholics have much to teach Protestants and all Jews and Christians perhaps, about reflection on the Bible. In the Synoptic Gospels, Jesus is a human being. In the Fourth Gospel he is God. Both God *and* a human being? Catholics ask: How can this be? And especially in our decades of the latter part of the twentieth century, Catholics are saying many bold, creative things about Jesus the "God man" which show that the old Christian teaching of the "Incarnation" of God, as it is called, is still open to examination. This is just an example of modern Catholic work in the theology of the Bible.

Lesson from Protestants

Protestants also do reverence to the Bible in their churches, often as earnestly as Jews or Eastern Christians do. And their theology is often as good as any Christian theology anywhere. But the thing we shall select to stress about Protestants and the Bible is how they emphasize the private reading of the Bible.

As we saw, the Gospels, like the rest of the New Testament, were all written to be read in the Church. The Old Testament, too, was written mostly for a like purpose—to be read aloud in the assembly of the People of God.

Private reading of the Bible? The ancients would have been astounded.

But we must remember, almost no one could read in those days. If an ancient Jew or Christian could step into a time-machine and come up to our day, and see a Protestant with a Bible in his or her lap, head bowed, eyes closed, a prayer on his or her lips, then head up again, eyes open, and continuing to read the word of God, silently, meditatively, perhaps that ancient Jew or Christian would not be shocked, as we might be tempted to think. Perhaps he or she would say with a smile, "Well, I never thought of that, but perhaps that's just the way it should be."